The Yellow Star

The Yellow Star

by

S. B. Unsdorfer

FELDHEIM PUBLISHERS

Jerusalem / New York

Library of Congress Catalog Number: 61-6930

First published 1961 by *Thomas Yoseloff*, New York & London
Second edition (paperback), by *Corgi Books*, London
Third edition, 1983
Hardcover: ISBN 0-87306-336-8
Paperback: ISBN 0-87306-337-6

Philipp Feldheim inc.
96 East Broadway
New York, NY 10002

Feldheim Publishers Ltd
POB 6525 / Jerusalem, Israel

Printed in Israel

For these I weep. Mine eye, mine eye runneth down with water, for comfort is far from me.

(Lamentations 1:17)

To the memory of my parents, grandparents, my sister, her husband and five young children, my uncles, aunts, and cousins, who, with six million of their brothers and sisters, were massacred by the Nazis.

CONTENTS

The Yellow Star

INTRODUCTION

WHO KNEW when the Second World War *really* started? Did it
start on September 3, 1939? Did it begin with Hitler's rise
to power, or did it start on the last day of World War I? Nobody could tell, least of all a boy of fourteen, whose only care
in the world was to make progress in school, and to beat his
pals in sports and games.

But when one Saturday afternoon in the late summer of
1939, I was attending our weekly Youth Club and we were
suddenly surrounded by a mob of wild drunkards who beat us
and kicked us out of our club rooms with a chorus of "Out
with the Jews!" I knew that a war was on. No gun had yet
been fired anywhere, no rifle raised—but I knew I was a Jew
and had been beaten for it.

The place where this happened has many names: "Bratislava," it is called by the Slovakian section of the population;
"Pressburg," insisted the German-speaking citizens; "Po-
zsony," lamented the Hungarians, the few faithful Magyars in
the city, who were still dreaming of the old days of the
Monarchy.

But I had a simpler name for it: I called it affectionately

HOME . . . the place where my mother and my five brothers and sisters were born, the town in which every cornerstone and every tramcar, every shop and every fruit-stall was "ours."

To Jews the world over, Bratislava was a familiar name. It represented a city which for generations had been headed by renowned rabbinical scholars whose Talmudic works have the force of law in matters of Jewish ritual, and whose names are revered throughout the world. It was known as a Jewish "mother community" which established schools and social institutions, homes for the aged, and hospitals for the sick which were the envy of many a larger and richer town.

My father was an integral part of this wonderful community. An ambitious, energetic, and learned rabbi, he grew in name and fame, and when World War II was launched by Hitler, he was one of the most beloved figures in the town. Much as his many admirers, young and old, clung to him, he clung to them even more closely. How else could he have let his American affidavit expire without using it? Position, house, and a great future were awaiting him in the United States of America; fares for the whole family were assured. All that he needed to do to save himself and his dear ones was to sit down and write a few words and cable them to the congregation in New York, pick up the visa at the American Embassy, and safety was his, and his family's.

But my father never wrote that cable and the words which might have saved his life, and my mother's. It would be wrong, he said, at this critical moment to desert his synagogue, his youth movement, and his friends. He saw to it, however, that my two older brothers, then aged nineteen and twenty, would get to England "so that their studies might not be interrupted," but for himself and the rest of us he was an optimist, an unshakable believer in the triumph of human rights and justice. He believed that we were all in God's hands, and that a Germany so recently defeated could not put up much opposition to a democratic world of united nations, bound by numerous pacts and defence agreements.

But then the real war started. Czechoslovakia was divided. Hitler occupied Prague, and Slovakia became an "independent" state with Bratislava its capital city. Poland was defeated, Holland and Belgium occupied, France beaten, but Father remained optimistic.

Even the reports of mass-murder and annihilation which reached us from Poland did not shatter his faith. Then came strict anti-Jewish measures at home: Jewish shops were "aryanised"; the "Yellow Star," six inches square, had to be worn; universities, cafes, hotels and holiday resorts were declared "out of bounds" for the Jews; one compartment in each train was reserved for "Jews Only," etc., etc. But Father remained firm. In his conversation, and particularly in his addresses from the pulpit, he described the calamities as an act of God, summoning us to return to Him and His Commandments.

By early 1942, the threat of deportation became really serious. Terror and fear descended upon us like a blanket of fog. But Father remained hopeful. "The Slovakian government is headed by Tiso, a Catholic priest," he would argue. "He could never allow deportation! No religious man would ever be party to it! The Vatican wouldn't permit it."

But by April, 1942, these hopes were shattered. The mass murder of Slovakian Jewry began at the rate of three thousand per week. First, transports of young girls only, followed by boys from sixteen onwards. They were sent to Auschwitz. And I? . . .

With a letter from a local doctor, I journeyed to Nitra, about 100 kilometers away, and spent three weeks in a hospital with the help of my two brothers-in-law. By May, deportations of entire families had begun, and I rejoined my parents at home to share my fate with them.

Only Jews "most essential for the economy of the state—

irreplaceable people" were given a white document exempting them from deportation. Father, being the spiritual head of the Burial Society, was thus granted exemption. But it followed that as thousands upon thousands of our townsmen were led to their deaths, the local Burial Society had little to do. Auschwitz became Jewry's cemetery, and the cattle wagons, their cortège. Father was still an optimist, but his faith was now tempered by events. I awoke one morning, in the very early hours, to find him throwing crumbs of bread to a few lonely pigeons on the windowsill. He was murmuring something. I sharpened my ears to catch his words. "Oh, merciful God!" he pleaded. "As I feed these innocent little birds—may You provide food and shelter to our starved and stricken brethren out there in the camps. Give them wings, like the birds, so that they may escape, and find refuge and rest."

Yes, his sermons were now directed to the One above, while his sympathy was with those below.

Months dragged by, months during which you saw your friends and neighbors, your grocer and teacher, your doctor and lawyer dragged away mercilessly to their deaths. In no time, Bratislava became an "orphan community" with only a few thousand escapees and "essential Jews" existing either in damp and smelly cellars, or in small and overcrowded rooms in the Ghetto streets.

As the wagons of the condemned rolled to the extermination camps, a small group of men and one woman met in secret conference. At the head sat Rabbi M. D. Weissmandel, a comparatively young but very capable and courageous man. "Gentlemen," he said, "if deportations are to continue at this rate, Slovakia will be without Jews in a matter of two or three months." Actually the rabbi had said nothing new. Every Jewish child was aware that there were by then less than thirty thousand Jews left in the country. Rabbi Weissmandel went on: "We have but one last chance to try and hold the deportations. . . . Let us get to Wisliczeni and offer him money!"

The members of the committee looked aghast at the young rabbi. Offer Wisliczeni a bribe? Herr von Wisliczeni, Adolph Eichmann's right-hand man? The most trusted Nazi in Slovakia? It was insane even to think of it, let alone dare to approach him.

Rabbi Weissmandel remained firm. He insisted that they had nothing to lose and everything to gain. "What can he do to us?" the Rabbi argued. "He cannot deport us twice, nor can he kill us twice! We *must* give it a try. We must make the offer so attractive and so tempting that even he will not reject it." Mrs. Gisi Fleischmann, the only woman on the committee, agreed with him.

A few nights later, a taxi stood silently in a blacked-out street, a few blocks away from Wisliczeni's office. In it sat four tense and worried members of the committee, anxiously awaiting the return of their spokesman from Wisliczeni. Minutes later their man joined them: "It seems all right," he whispered. "He wants to discuss it with Eichmann. . . . If Eichmann agrees, he will take fifty thousand dollars in cash, in two instalments."

A fortnight later, a paper parcel containing twenty-five thousand dollars, the first of the two instalments, was placed on Wisliczeni's desk, and the wagons were halted. He allowed the Jews a "truce" of six weeks, by which time the remaining twenty-five thousand dollars were to be paid.

These were hectic weeks, but despite their superhuman efforts, the committee was unable to raise the full amount. Two days after the expiration of the time limit, Wisliczeni ordered the immediate deportation of three thousand Jews. That was on the eve of Yom Kippur, 1942. Forty-eight hours after Yom Kippur, with three thousand Jews inside their wagons but still on Slovakian soil, the remaining twenty-five thousand dollars were given to Wisliczeni. "Aha!" he jeered as he took the par-

[15]

cel. "You thought that you could stall payment until the war was over and then keep both the money and your people. Well, I will teach you to trade with me! The three thousand people must go!"

Indeed the way in which these few heroic men managed to raise fifty thousand dollars in six weeks in a country under the terror of the Nazis is a story in itself, an eventful and tragic chapter in Jewish history. Suffice it to say that through the extraordinary courage, skill, and self-sacrifice of these men, no further deportations from Slovakia took place after the autumn of 1942. The few thousand remaining Jews spent the next year in their ghetto homes in comparative safety, though never without fear.

When Germany's fronts began to crumble, our hopes slowly rose. The heavy drone of Allied aircraft flying night after night over Bratislava was accompanied by our good wishes and our ardent prayers.

As 1944 advanced, our chances of survival grew with it. The war was now a race between good and evil, between life and death. Russian troops were fighting in the streets of Hungary; the Allies were knocking at the doors of Germany. "The Germans will have no time to worry over us," my father ventured hopefully. . . .

All this changed when Slovakian partisans began their uprising. At first we thought that this would bring the end even closer. Hundreds of surviving Jews joined the partisans in the Carpathian hills. But then, one night in August, 1944, thousands of German troops crossed the bridge over the Danube, to occupy Bratislava and the entire country. The *Wehrmacht* disarmed the Slovakian army, the Gestapo replaced the police, and the S.S. took charge of the few remaining Jews.

In despair, my parents and I escaped to an old castle in the nearby village of Mariathal. . . .

And that is where my own fearful story begins.

I BRATISLAVA AND SERED

IT WAS about 11 A.M. on October 11, 1944, the day after *Simhat Torah*, when I stood in the chilly wind on the dew-covered lawn of an old castle near Bratislava, the capital of Slovakia. I began to walk, not for pleasure, but simply because there was nothing else I could do. I covered the short distance of the lawn and then reversed myself and walked back. Not for me the world outside the castle gardens: I was an internee, but only a fake one. Indeed, we were all fakes—all the Jews who herded together in this ancient fortress.

For safety's sake we had faked the Argentine passports which brought my parents and me to this Bratislavian castle because these documents entitled us to an internment under police regulations: an uneasy, suspense-filled internment, to be sure, but one which was preferable to being "free" and at large in a country where everyone's hand was raised against our race.

The war was nearing its end, and the majority of Slovakian Jews had already been deported to German concentration camps during the mass deportations which had taken place in 1942. However, in the latter half of 1944, the few thousand

Jews who had been permitted to remain in the country (on the grounds that they were required for the economic needs of the State) were driven to desperate measures by increasing fears that the Germans, harried by disruptive partisan activity and sabotage, would totally occupy Slovakia.

This handful of Jews, who through a hundred and one miracles had hitherto managed to escape deportation, decided to supply themselves with false South American passports, and on the strength of these, prevail upon the Slovakian puppet government to intern them as foreigners and keep them under its protection until the war was ended.

My father, in his middle fifties, my mother, a few years older, and I, who was nineteen, were among these phony Argentines. The generous dispensation of money eventually convinced the Slovakian police that we were genuine South American nationals and should be interned as such. Thus, on September 20, 1944, one day after *Rosh Hashanah,* and about three weeks after German troops had occupied the country, my parents and I, together with a small number of other families, moved into the old castle in Mariathal, near Bratislava, where we were placed under constant police guard.

We all knew that we were gambling with death, and every time we watched German military police in the vicinity of the castle and saw them questioning the police officers at the gate, we quailed at the slender barrier we had erected to protect ourselves, but we were heartened again and again by the knowledge that the Nazis had never yet attempted to enter and question the internees. As the days dragged on, our hopes rose. Would our trick confound the astute war machine of Hitler?

By *Yom Kippur* there were about 180 people in the castle— men, women, and children. I remember the services conducted on *Yom Kippur* in one of the castle rooms, and the sermon which my father, who was a rabbi, delivered before *Mazkir* (memorial service for the dead).

"Call them all in," he told me gently, ". . . even those who have forsaken our religion and no longer believe in prayer."

They all came, and never shall I forget the short parable with which my father illustrated his sermon. Everyone was in tears: that was what he wanted to achieve. "The gates of tears never close," say our rabbis. "If nothing reaches the ears of God, the tears of the innocent will always find Him."

My father was a tall, dignified man, ever ready to help and comfort his fellow men. He was a born leader. As I watched the sad expression on the lined face of my mother, and saw how frail she had grown with the ceaseless anxieties of the last five years, I wondered how she would survive a worsening of our perilous position. My brothers and sisters were older than I. I had never been away from home and was extremely attached to my family. I wondered then how long it would be before we were torn apart.

Yom Kippur had been celebrated, and into the uneasy silence that followed came the news that we all had dreaded. German troops, who had occupied the entire country some weeks earlier and had brought with them large detachments of Gestapo and S.S. men, had made a sudden swoop on all Jews in Bratislava and had made the capital *"Judenrein."* The helpless prisoners were herded into the detention camp in Sered. One or two fugitives had managed to reach us, and we had offered them slender sanctuary in the castle, for as they had no documents, they would be immediately discovered should there be an inspection; and that inspection, we felt, was bound to come in the very near future.

New fears and tensions were born during the next two or three days, for after the arrest of the Jews in the capital, we were certain the S.S. would come in search of us. But, as the days went by, and the Festival of *Sukkot* approached, we were

[21]

once again lulled into a false sense of security and began to build up our shaken morale. It was not possible, we argued, that the Germans were not aware of our being here. If they really wanted us they could have already collected us along with the rest of the Slovakian Jews.

And so the Jewish festivals, including *Sukkot* (one of the Festivals of the Tabernacles), passed by without alarm. This was the only *Sukkot* during the six years of war that we had neither a *Sukkah* (a booth erected for the Feast of Tabernacles) nor an *Etrog* nor a *Lulav* (requisites for religious services).

Even in the darkest months of 1942, when Jews were shipped to Auschwitz by the thousand, we had a tiny hut hidden in the back of our garden which we used as a *Sukkah*. In that year there was only one *Etrog* and *Lulav* for the whole Jewish community of Slovakia. A trusty gentile was asked to tour the Jewish communities by car with this one set of *Arbaah Minim*, and congregants were informed beforehand at what day and hour they had to assemble in the synagogue in order to have a chance of making the blessing on the *Arbaah Minim*. But on this *Sukkot* in 1944, we had nothing but the memories of all our previous experiences.

Thus, on the day following the festival, October 11, I found myself strolling in the beautiful gardens surrounding the castle, with their tall elegant oak trees and lovely flower beds. I had left my father in his room, after having tried everything possible to keep myself occupied. Father had a six-year-old boy on his lap and was teaching him the *Aleph Bet* (Hebrew alphabet). On the previous day my father had undertaken to spend the whole day teaching adults and children—in fact everyone who wanted to have a lesson was welcome to join him.

My mother was with a number of other women in the huge communal kitchen in the basement where the first kosher meal cooked on the premises was to be prepared. Fish was on the menu. There was no longer any kosher meat because the ritual slaughterers and the kosher butchers had been deported.

I paused in my perambulations at the sound of distant commotion, and to my horror saw that the whole place was surrounded by S.S. men. At the front entrance an S.S. bus and three Mercedes cars drew up, and as I turned round it seemed there was an S.S. man with revolver in hand behind almost every tree. We were besieged!

I raced into the castle, taking the steps two at a time until I reached my father.

"Papa," I cried. "They're here . . . all over the place."

I was in a panic, as I always was in those years when I had to face a German uniform. The mere sight of a swastika, whether on a flagpole or on a badge, made me freeze with terror.

My father rushed to the window. How glad I was that he no longer wore his rabbinical garb, and that his short but very attractive beard did not reveal his profession. He had been reluctant to part with the traditional apparel and beard of his vocation, but on the firm advice of many trusted friends, he had shorn his beard and changed into a gray suit a few days before we moved into the castle.

How the S.S. would have enjoyed catching a rabbi! I shudder to think what they would have done to him. Now he looked like a well-to-do company director, much younger than his fifty-five years.

"Quickly," he ordered, "get Mama up from the kitchen!"

I sped to do his bidding, but I met Mother on the halfway landing. She looked pale and worried, but her calmness conquered my immediate panic.

"They have come to check our passports," she said as we walked together upstairs.

Back in my father's room we paced up and down nervously, occasionally glancing out of the window. People were now beginning to queue up on the lawn. We waited fatalistically for our turn, which came only too soon.

The castle trembled under the weight of a crowd of burly S.S. men who raced up to the top floor shouting wildly: "Everybody downstairs! Everybody!"

By now they were all over the castle—on the staircase, in the hall, on the roof, in the cellar, and about the garden. The two castle police officers were confined to their rooms. We were entirely in the hands of the dreaded S.S.

It took them only a few minutes to get the whole 180 of us—men, women and children—lined up on the first floor landing. An S.S. officer, who I later learned was the notorious *Hauptsturmfuehrer* Anton Brunner, who had been sent to Slovakia with the occupying troops to "take charge" of the Jews, was seated behind an empty desk—two S.S. men, revolvers ready, standing behind him.

Brunner, the Commandant of the reception camp in Sered, and of many other concentration camps previously, was a slim, saturnine figure with fair hair and a temper as quick as mercury. He had long, prehensile, apelike fingers which looked as though they itched to be round our throats. His long face wore a perpetually cynical expression, and his gimlet eyes knew no mercy.

As I watched him, the smell of freshly cooked fish from the deserted kitchen engulfed the entire building. The first kosher meal—which no one was to touch, incidentally—was almost ready to be served. Brunner smiled sardonically, unable to hide his pleasure and delight at the sight of 180 newly discovered "political criminals," while we waited quietly and patiently upon his every word.

"Passkontrolle," he said calmly with that hateful, cynical smile on his long, haggard face.

One by one we showed this savage our passports: Argentine, Bolivian, Brazilian, Cuban, etc. A woman of about forty stood in front of us. She was shaking with fear and worry as she approached him.

"*Bitte*," she pleaded desperately. "Please, *mein Herr,* my American passport is deposited with the police at Topolcany . . . I can get it in a day or two . . . it is a genuine and valid passport, and I would . . ."

Brunner cut in with his everlasting smirk. "That's all right. We'll get your passport for you. If it's valid and in order, you'll have nothing to worry about."

She was showering him with words of thanks and gratitude when Brunner nodded his head curtly and said to the S.S. man behind him: "See that the 'lady' queues up downstairs." He emphasized the word *lady.*

Now it was our turn. My father stepped forward, calm and apparently unmoved by this Nazi terror. He bade Brunner a kindly good-morning, and handed over his passport.

"*Sprechen Sie Spanisch?*" Brunner asked, after glancing at the passport.

"No," answered my father without hesitation.

"Queue up downstairs!" Brunner ordered, and put the passport on the pile that was slowly growing on his desk.

Next came my mother's ordeal, and then my own.

It took Brunner less than half an hour to get through the whole line of internees. Now and again he flew into a temper, particularly when someone answered his question with, "Yes, I do speak Spanish!" This seemed to infuriate him, and without attempting to test the truth of the statement, he would jump from his seat screaming: "You dirty liar; get in the queue downstairs before I use the gun on you!"

No one dared argue with him; it would have been of no help, anyway.

When the last family had marched downstairs, we were ordered to line up once more and stand five deep. We were filled with apprehension and grim forebodings. What would happen next?

We were completely encircled by S.S. men while Brunner paced up and down the line as if taking a salute on parade. Carefully he counted and recounted his catch. His temper was forgotten. Once again he expressed his pleasure and delight by baring his teeth in a wide, jubilant smile, and by rubbing his hands gleefully. Obviously he was deriving keen enjoyment from torturing us by making it clear that our fate was entirely in his hands, that we were all at his mercy, and that his every word could mean life or death to us. He paused sometimes as if about to speak, then he would change his mind and recount us.

Brunner kept us waiting in this torture for minute after minute. He well knew how to tauten suspense and heighten tension until they became almost unbearable.

All this time we stood stiffly at attention while he examined each one of us closely, boring into our eyes as if he were going to wrest our poor secrets from us by sheer will power.

Then quite suddenly he moved a few steps backwards and shouted: "You have fifteen minutes to get packed. Don't take too many things with you because you'll have to walk eight kilometers to the nearest railway station at Stupava."

I looked at my father. As always in these years of terror and panic, he kept cool and calm, reassuring us of his complete faith in the Almighty as Savior and Guardian of His people.

"We'd better put on two shirts and double underwear," he advised, as we got back into our room. "It will make our luggage lighter, and anyway they will surely not take away what is on our bodies."

We dressed quickly. Father took down his rucksack and put in his *Tallit* and *Tefillin;* Mother took her candlesticks and a packet of candles for the Sabbath lights; I filled mine with food and fruit and all the cigarettes that we had stored in our cupboard.

Within fifteen minutes the whole troop of S.S. re-invaded the house and threw out everyone who was not completely ready. Some came down in their shirtsleeves, and some without coats or hats, but everyone obeyed the fifteen-minute order and stood stiffly at attention awaiting the next move of the fiend who would determine their destinies.

ONCE AGAIN we stood five deep; once again Brunner marched up and down the line to take yet another count. His apelike fingers were curling and uncurling in growing irritation.

"Confound these children!" he screamed at the top of his voice. "They are not standing still. I can't get my numbers right."

Desperately, harrowed parents pulled their children into line. These poor youngsters were getting restless; they were tired and puzzled by all the excitement and the panic around them. It was a mercy they did not understand the dark tragedy that encircled them; they wanted their dinner and their afternoon sleep. . . . Beyond that, they had no further thought.

Brunner took another count, and then another. Finally, he burst out with a wild yell: "One person missing!"

His fury was so wild that even the S.S. men looked alarmed. They raced back into the castle in a mad rush to scoop up the unfortunate fugitive. We stood, too deep in our own fears to consider the fate of the luckless absent one.

Then we saw the S.S. men dragging a thin man by his hair.

"Found him hiding under some straw," reported the proud captor. Brunner had no time for compliments: "What's your name?" he demanded of the prisoner.

"Haar."

Brunner forced him into the line with a foul kick in the stomach. Haar got up. "Please, may I collect some of my things?"

"No!" screamed Brunner. "You go without anything—you'll help others carry their bags or their children."

Haar was in his shirtsleeves, a slender, by no means unintelligent man of about forty-five. Indeed, he was one of the originators of the internment idea. If Brunner had known, he would have shot him on the spot. Haar knew what he was doing. He did not wish to aggravate his master; he might need him again—as indeed he did.

No sooner was that little drama over, than another S.S. man appeared from the castle dragging a young boy.

"Who was this?" we all thought. We hadn't seen the boy before. We feared for his fate.

The S.S. man came smartly to attention, clapped his jackboots together, and reported: "Found the boy on the window sill in the attic!"

"Who are you?" asked the *Hauptsturmfuehrer*, as a deathly silence fell.

"Steiner!" came the boyish treble.

"How old are you?"

"Twelve."

"Where are your parents?"

The boy hesitated. It would not have mattered whom he had pretended to identify in the crowd, for they would have stood by the lad. Brunner knew no names—not yet, anyway. But the child would not know that. He could have said that his parents were already deported—any answer would have been better than the one he chose to give.

"Don't know!" he ventured.

Brunner felled him with one quick blow on the ear. "*Where are your parents?*" he stormed.

"My father is hiding in Bratislava," the child confessed. "My mother isn't here any more."

"What is your father?" Brunner's questions leapt one after the other.

"A doctor."

"Do you know where he is now?"

"Yes," the child answered, tears rolling down his pale cheeks.

"Here!" Brunner turned to an S.S. man. "Get into a car and bring his father here. The boy will show you the way."

That cost us a further hour of tense waiting. It was not until well after three in the afternoon that young Steiner and his panic-stricken father were brought back to the castle and ordered into line. This necessitated a further count, but it was the final one for the day. Brunner stationed himself in front of the group, rather like a headmaster about to address an assembly on the school ground, and declared:

"You will march to the nearest railway station and from there be taken by train to Sered. There is no chance of escape! Anyone attempting to run, or even leave the line, will be shot without warning! Keep your children well in line—if you want them to stay alive. . . . *Auf Wiedersehn!*" he shouted gleefully and returned to his car.

Escorted on both sides by S.S. men, we began our fateful march, watched by a handful of old villagers, and followed by the sickening smell of burnt fish. . . .

In front of my father, mother, and me, marched Alexander Eckstein and his young wife. He was a short, skinny man who until the outbreak of the war had been a promising young journalist. His professional life had brought him into close contact with the police, and when he was sacked from his newspaper because of his Jewish descent, he made use of his connections with the police to help his fellow men who had been taken into custody for breaking one or the other of the endless number of anti-Jewish regulations. Eckstein was liked and respected for his selfless and risky work during these war years. He appeared to have recognized one of the escorting S.S. men as a former policeman, and slowed down in his march until he came to walk side by side with him.

"Please?" he whispered. "You know who I am. Give me a chance to save my life. . . . Please help me."

"Shut up," yelled the S.S. man at the top of his voice. "If I see you step out of this line, I'll empty my gun on you."

Eckstein was not taken aback by this exhibition of power and superiority. He had experienced it too often in the past, and knew how to handle these beasts. In any case he had little to lose by persisting in his questions.

"And if you don't see me, will you fire?" he ventured quietly.

The S.S. man spoke more normally.

"If I don't see you I can't kill you—can I?"

"Well, you don't *have* to see me, do you?" suggested Eckstein.

The S.S. man did not answer, and Eckstein was satisfied. He whispered to his wife and told her to start running as soon as he pulled her arm. But she would not listen. Her courage had evaporated. Brunner's grim warning was still ringing in her ears, and she did not trust these S.S. men. Husband and wife argued on. . . .

Behind me walked Benzion Gottlieb, a well-built, corpulent man of about forty, accompanied by his attractive blonde wife and their two children. I pitied them. They should not have been here marching with us. Benzi, as we called him later, had joined us in Mariathal only three days ago. While Bratislava was made *Judenrein*, he and his family were tucked

[31]

away safely in a bunker outside the town. He had a Salvadorian passport and could have been with us in the castle, but he was not a great believer in the internment idea and preferred the safety of his own bunker. However, when he heard that Brunner had left Mariathal untouched he had second thoughts. It was very difficult to remain in a bunker for a lengthy period without being able to talk to anyone, with no contacts, indefinitely shut away from the whole world. He had to think of his children. How could they spend months and months in hiding without giving the show away? He had written to my father asking him whether he should join us in the castle. Father's reply was very brief. He could not advise him on so difficult a question; all he could assure him was that we were still safe and unharmed in the castle.

Next day Benzi arrived outside the castle grounds in a taxi. He was very optimistic when he came, though he reported that the taxi had been stopped twice by the Gestapo. He showed them his passport and explained that he was an internee at Mariathal. They were satisfied and allowed him to pass.

Benzi's report had spelled good news for all of us. We too became more confident about the future—that is, until the morning when Brunner and his henchmen arrived. . . .

We had not been marching more than an hour when trouble started. The pace proved too much for the children, and even some of the older ones had to be carried now and again. The experiences of the morning, the weight of the rucksacks, plus the children, brought many to near collapse. Some of the marchers, particularly women, developed diarrhea from the shock and emotions of the day. But the S.S. beasts would not allow any pause, nor would they permit individuals to relieve themselves under the cover of trees or hedges. It was "ten steps sideways and one minute's time." They enjoyed with great glee the humiliation and embarrassment of their victims.

It was well after nightfall when we approached the railway

station. When we had come to within a few hundred yards of it, Eckstein and his wife were still arguing about escape. He was trying desperately to revive her courage, but this only made her even more distraught. Then in a flash Eckstein dropped his rucksack and ducked into a hedge just as we turned a narrow corner at the station's approach.

Did the S.S. man see him? We shall never know. Eckstein was lucky, and his luck held. He escaped with the assistance of the Swiss Red Cross, and after the war was rejoined by his wife, who had returned from the concentration camp after liberation.

But alas! the Ecksteins were the exception rather than the rule. For the rest, there was little chance of escape, and only a few of the 180 of us managed to survive.

There was a considerable waiting period at the station, and because of the poor light provided by the old-fashioned gas lamps, the S.S. men were particularly strict and vigilant. Eventually two empty coaches chugged in lazily, pulled by an old engine. The whole 179 of us—Eckstein was gone—were crammed into these two coaches. The S.S. posted themselves at the doors at both ends, barring our way even to the toilets. Then the train moved off.

It was not the first time that I left Stupava in a packed train. At one time, Stupava was a popular picnic spot, whose beautiful woods and romantic canoe lake attracted many a youngster out for a Sunday excursion. In those days, the fuller the train, the merrier our homegoing. But those happy days had gone forever—days when the Jew enjoyed the same rights and privileges, the same natural delights as his gentile neighbor. How everything had changed! The notice "Danger! Political Prisoners!" was splashed on every compartment.

Somberly we crouched in silence, not even daring to think. Father sat at the window facing the engine, Mother on the seat opposite, and I sat on the floor between them. What a pitiful sight it was compared with the last occasion I had travelled with them on this very line. Mother had left her warm scarf in the castle and the draft from the ill-fit window distressed her greatly. When we were just about to go over the "Red Bridge," Father gave a reassuring nod to her.

Who among us did not know the "Red Bridge"? It was at this spot where passengers would normally rise from their seats, pull their luggage from the racks, and get ready to step out happily at Bratislava. The "Red Bridge" was part of Bratislava; to us it was part of what we affectionately called home. But this time nobody moved, for the train showed no signs of stopping. Our luggage and the rucksacks remained firmly on the racks, unheeded.

Mother looked down into the peaceful river as if to bid farewell to an old and valued friend. She was obviously moved. Father, as if reading her thoughts, interrupted her:

"Mammele," he said tenderly. "Shall we go in by tramcar or shall I hire a taxi?"

That is the question he would normally have asked as the train reached the Red Bridge, which was situated about one kilometer from the station. It was meant to be a joke to cheer her up, but it failed. She looked straight into my father's face, sighed deeply, but no sound came from her trembling lips. She fought bravely to keep back her tears. But when the train roared past her birthplace, her tears rolled down fast. It was goodbye Bratislava. . . . Goodbye to the house and home. . . . Goodbye to them forever.

Late in the evening our train stopped at Leopoldov, one of Slovakia's major railway junctions. The S.S. quickly surrounded the two coaches and ordered everyone to remain seated until the train moved again. "Anyone attempting to get up will be shot immediately!" they yelled.

For two or three hours our coaches were shunted from siding to siding. Large-scale troop movements took place throughout the night, and our little train must have been in the way. Again and again shots were fired—the bullets screamed past our windows—to scare us and make sure that no one would move.

My feet were like lead from sitting in a cramped position all these hours. Father wanted to change seats, but I would not allow this. In any case, who would risk a bullet just for the sake of getting a more comfortable seat?

Finally the train moved slowly off again. To where? And why?

LIKE MOST Slovakian cities, Sered had a fairly large Jewish population with its synagogues, Jewish schools, and Talmudical college. In short, it was a flourishing Jewish community, a pleasant little town. But that was Sered of old.

The new Sered spelled terror to every Jew. In 1942, the city was chosen to serve as a reception center for Jewish deportees, and it seemed almost overnight that a concentration camp appeared with its barbed-wire fences, watchtowers, and all the horrors inseparable from these bestial cages. The local Jews fled in panic to other cities in the hope that they might escape the dragnet which would haul them into the camp.

The normal practice of the deportations was to gather together each week a batch of a thousand Jews and transport them to Auschwitz. Sered was the depot into which they were herded in ones and twos until the required number was reached and ready for dispatch. The Jews living in Sered were in particular danger, because if the Germans were short by two or three hundred, they could always turn to the local Jews at the very last moment and complete their batches. Sered was one stop before Auschwitz—one step nearer to death.

This we all knew as we sat in that train, rolling towards our doom.

Although Sered is only about ten kilometers from Leopoldov, we were confined to our compartments until after daybreak, when unloading began. Yes, indeed, unloading: from the moment of our arrival at Sered we ceased to be human beings and became part of a huge consignment of European Jewry destined for delivery to the Auschwitz extermination camp, by order of Hitler.

None of us had slept that night; even the little children had failed to succumb to natural fatigue. Now came the moment of alighting. Accompanied by constant reminders by the S.S. men for speed—quicker, faster, quicker—we stood five deep in the cold and misty October morning for the count to be taken. Then it was march, quick march, to the camp. Mercifully it took but a few minutes, for they had built a special railway line leading to the camp, no doubt to make last-minute escapes impossible. Then the huge barbed gates were thrown open by two S.S. men to admit the "newcomers."

We saw the Jews already in the camp hurry to their doors and windows, watching with horror as another column of their brethren were marched in. Another batch for Auschwitz! Who are they? they would be wondering, trying to distinguish our features and praying that they would not recognize one of their own family.

As the huge gates shut behind us a feeling of utter despair filled me. The gaunt rows of huts and the tangle of barbed wire; the grim towers from which, night and day, the eagle-eyes of the S.S. watched and watched, guns ready to mow us down; the huge mirrors of searchlights ready to flood out their blinding light through the long night, should there be any disturbance; the cruel-faced guards everywhere: this was our destiny.

The camp police, consisting of young Jewish boys, some of them my former schoolmates, lined us up at once in front of an S.S. officer. Without expression he recorded particulars: the names, former addresses, dates of birth, occupation, etc. of each one of us. It was not until eleven A.M. on Thursday morning, exactly twenty-four hours after our capture in the castle at Mariathal, that we were allowed into the barracks for a rest.

I stayed but a few minutes with my parents, and then I left the barracks for a cautious exploration of our cage. My first object was to try to establish the number of inmates interned in this particular camp. To my great horror I soon learned that the previous day a transport of a thousand people had been sent to Auschwitz which included my eldest sister, Ilonka, her husband, Romi, and their five small children. Dear Ilonka! She was the favorite of all of us. I loved her deeply, and was so afraid of the effect on my parents' morale if they heard of her fate, that I decided not to be the one to tell them the tragic news. Now that this batch had left, I learned that there were only about 300 people who remained in the camp, excluding 150 police, kitchen and barracks staff, mixed marriage couples, and hospital patients who had hitherto not been included in any of the transports. The significance of this number was not lost upon me. It meant that together with his latest catch of Mariathal Jews, Brunner had only about five hundred victims, even taking into consideration that he would doubtless cut the number of police and general staff. We were thus quite safe for the time being. Brunner had collected his last big catch from Mariathal; otherwise the whole of the country was *Judenrein*—except for those who hid in their bunkers or accommodated themselves with non-Jewish families who offered them shelter at tremendous risk to themselves.

[38]

That first night there was a terrible commotion in the camp. The Jewish police barrack was surrounded by S.S. men, and then shrieks, groans, and cries of terror echoed, and panic spread, throughout the camp. It was impossible to get news, for everyone lay or sat petrified with fear wondering what new terror would at any moment descend upon him to swell the sound of suffering. After quiet had come to us, we dozed fitfully until the next morning, when to our alarm we found a number of young policemen walking about with bandaged heads or arms, with black eyes and swollen mouths. What had happened? The explanation came in all its stark horror. These Jews were told when they signed on as camp policemen that they and their wives would not be deported until the very last transport. Consequently, several of them had volunteered to register one of the many young girls in the camp as a "policeman's wife" and thus save her from early deportation. That night, Brunner, with his usual cynicism, had decided to make a check on the "married" Jewish policemen. He swooped down on the police barrack to find out if they were sleeping with their "wives." Every policeman who was caught sleeping alone was beaten up brutally by the half-drunk S.S. men and told that he would be included in the next transport.

The atmosphere in the camp grew more tense as the day progressed. Nobody dared leave his barrack. At about nine o'clock, a swollen-faced policeman entered our barrack and came to my father. Father comforted him.

"Even if you have saved this girl from deportation for only a few weeks," he told the young man, "it may eventually mean that you have saved her life. You may rest assured that reward for your heroic deed and for your decency will be forthcoming."

But the policeman, although he appreciated it, had not come to ask for comfort. He handed Father a letter saying:

"The Commandant grants you permission to read this letter,

but has ordered that it be given back within fifteen minutes, together with full name and address of the sender."

I quailed as I recognized the handwriting. It was a letter from my sister, Golda, who with her husband and baby was hiding in a bunker in nearby Nitra. Worse still, my other sister, Paula, with her husband and two children, was also in the same bunker, and they had sent us their usual daily letter to our castle address in Mariathal. There was, of course, no sender's address either on the envelope or in the letter.

"I was afraid of this," Father said gravely, as he began to read the letter.

"How did it get here?" I asked nervously.

"As we marched away from the castle," Father explained, "I noticed that when Brunner was returning to his car a postman arrived at the castle gates. Brunner took possession of his entire mailbag. And now, of course, he wants to lay his hands on the senders."

Mother hid her face and began to cry softly. Ever since deportations began in 1942, my three sisters, all of whom lived in Nitra, had written a letter home every day. They were not long letters, but for us the information they contained was more than important. They usually finished with the lines— "We and the children are well, and hope to hear the same from you." My sister Golda's present letter contained little more except that they all hoped we had spent the Festival as joyfully as could be expected under the circumstances, and that they were very worried about the well-being of Ilonka and her children.

"We musn't give them away," my mother pleaded. "Oh, my poor children. God knows how they manage to exist in that dark and damp cellar all these days. . . ."

"Of course we shan't give them away," Father comforted her. "We shall just write down their names and their old home

[40]

address. How are we to know where they have gone from there?"

"But supposing Brunner finds out?" I ventured. "You saw how quickly he brought in Dr. Steiner after bullying his young son. He will spare no effort to net Golda and Paula."

"We must hope and pray that he will not find out," answered Father calmly. "We shall not disclose their whereabouts no matter what means of torture Brunner applies. Our lips must remain sealed. . . ."

No sooner was this little trying moment over, and the letter with the name of my sister and her old address handed over to the policeman, than yet another policeman entered the barrack block calling for young volunteers to help with some clearing work. I hated the word "volunteers" and distrusted it. Far too many traps were disguised in that genial sounding word. I could not forget the call for volunteers during the 1942 deportations, when an order was issued inviting young men to report for work on the railways to protect themselves from deportation. Hundreds of eager young people left their hiding places and joined the "work for the railways" call. One night, just ten weeks after extremely heavy work in track-laying, it happened to be *Tisha B'Av*. As everyone sat down to the *Ekhah*, there was a sudden seizure of all the railway "volunteers," and they were packed off to Auschwitz overnight!

But there was also another logical reason for my reluctance to volunteer. I was afraid of being separated from my parents. As long as we stayed together, life was easier. Father's wonderful spirit, his deep-felt conviction that we were in God's hands, his unshakable belief that all would ultimately turn out for the good, made me feel safer and more secure. Of course, I realized that in the circumstances now facing us all, the days of our being together were limited, yet I wanted to make sure of being with them as long as I possibly could.

To my dismay, Father insisted on my going out to work.

"What if they find you here?" he said. "What if they find a young man of your age trying to dodge work? The atmosphere is too tense. You'd better not become involved in any further questioning."

So it was that I left the barrack together with a number of others. We were taken behind the camp buildings to huge piles of "leftovers." There must have been thousands of objects on every pile: coats, jackets, trousers, wallets, mirrors, combs, photographs, shoes, hats, handbags, toys, and tools left over by the people of the previous transport. These were to be sorted out and any valueless rubbish thrown into two huge bonfires.

I began to pile up the hardware onto one heap, picking out knives, forks, tin-plates, etc. I picked out these things with my hands and placed them on a heap behind me. Suddenly an S.S. man bore down upon me. A cold shiver ran down my spine at this first personal encounter with an S.S. man.

"Here," he said politely, "you'll get your fingers cut if you poke about in that pile bare-handed. Find yourself an old pair of gloves, or get a little stick in your hands."

"*Danke schoen,*" I said gratefully. "Thank you for being so kind."

I picked up a little stick and went on with my job, conscious of an overwhelming relief. "They are not so bad after all," I thought to myself. "Once they know that they have got you, they treat you differently."

I had hardly been at my job five minutes when that very same S.S. man came marching back to me. "Hey!" he yelled. "Can't you use your dirty fingers? Are they too good for this kind of work? Throw that stick away before I push it down your throat."

"*Jawohl,*" I said obediently, and flung the stick back into the pile. My brain was paralyzed. How could anyone survive such calculated sadism, such treachery? I asked myself as the

S.S. man turned away from me with a broad grin splitting his face. How can you avoid punishment if you don't know what to do?

I had a feeling that that particular S.S. man was going to have another go at me, so I decided to leave the pile and go to look after the unattended bonfire. I picked up a huge iron poker, flung a few books and other things on it, and poked the fire into a new blaze. In the distance I saw Brunner himself approaching. He carried what looked like a silver hammer, about six inches long, which he swung about playfully.

I froze. To what use would that elegant hammer be put? I breathed again as he stopped and fixed his gaze on a man working on a pile of old clothing.

"Tired?" I heard him inquire with mock politeness.

"A little," replied the man, falling at once into the trap.

"Lazy?" Brunner suggested smoothly.

"No, sir," said the man, paling. "I have worked all my life."

Brunner's face grew red. He turned to an S.S. man and shouted: "Give him some work to do."

The poor fellow was ordered to pick up two heavy stones weighing about twenty pounds each, and to run around in circles holding them. Every time he slowed down or dropped one of the stones he was beaten up by one of the three S.S. men who had joined Brunner in the "sport."

"Faster! Faster!" they yelled at him. They kicked him and knocked him about with their rifles until he collapsed to the ground.

"Now, perhaps, he does feel a little tired," joked Brunner. "Get the 'mess' cleared away from here," he ordered, and the Jewish police were summoned to carry the victim into the barrack on a stretcher.

I poked wildly into the fire, shivering like a jelly, and praying that I would not be the next victim. Then as I saw Brunner coming towards me I gathered all my will power to stop the ague that was attacking me.

A tap on my shoulder from his silver hammer brought me to attention.

"*Jawohl, Herr Hauptsturmfuehrer,*" I said loudly as I pulled off my cap.

"You clumsy fool," he yelled. "Do you expect the fire to burn if you throw thick closed books on it?"

"No, sir."

"Then get the books out of that bonfire."

"But the flames . . ." I panicked.

"You lousy coward," Brunner screamed as he pushed me aside. He stretched out his arm with its ugly long fingers, and pulled out a smouldering book. He held it open by its covers and threw it back into the fire. "That's the way to burn books."

"*Jawohl,*" I said, quietly.

"I will be back here in fifteen minutes," he warned. "I want to see nothing but ashes . . . or you'll go on the heap to help it burn!"

"Fifteen minutes!" I whispered to myself as Brunner left me to find yet another victim. "This pile will take hours to burn out, even if I pour petrol on it." I looked round frantically. I wanted to make a break for it, hide somewhere, or get back into the barracks. But there were too many S.S. men about.

I was saved by the bell. It was getting dark, and work had to stop, for the ringing of the camp bell ordered everyone back into the barracks on penalty of death. The police lined us up and marched us back. I lit a cigarette, drawing as deeply as I could, to restore my nerves a little, and to avoid meeting my parents in such a tense condition. Even so, I walked into our "room" shaking in every limb. The room was as small as a train compartment, with a couple of two-tiered bunks on each side and a tiny table in the middle. I stood there for a moment with my cigarette, half dazed. Until I saw my mother's two Sabbath candles flickering sadly on the naked table, and my father with his prayer book in his hand, I had completely forgotten that it was Friday evening, and that the Sabbath had come in.

Quickly I threw the cigarette away. "I am sorry," I said, with tears in my eyes. "I forgot . . ."

"Good *Shabbos,* my child," said Father gently. "Don't worry; it's not really nightfall yet; you still have a few minutes to wash your hands and face, and change your shirt in honor of the Sabbath."

I left the room as Father whispered the traditional Sabbath songs bidding the Angels of God to join the festive table laid out in honor of the Holy Sabbath.

"Welcome, oh Angels of God, to the bare and empty Sabbath tables of Thy servants in Concentration Camp Sered."

I wondered what would happen to us before the next Sabbath came in.

4

ALL WAS quiet in the camp that Saturday morning—*Sabbath Bereshit*—but it was an uneasy quiet that even the brightly shining sun did nothing to dissipate, though we were grateful enough that this October morning had not the chill we expected.

Sered was not a big camp compared with those which I had the misfortune to see in later months. There were no more than twenty-five wooden barracks, each housing about eighty internees. In addition, there were a number of workshops used for compulsory labor during the two years between autumn, 1942 and autumn, 1944, when there were no deportations. A hospital had been built in 1941, when the new and very modern Jewish Hospital in Bratislava was "taken over" by the Slovak authorities. The wire fences hemming in the camp were not electrified, and families were allowed to live together in one barrack, if not alone in one room or compartment. The food was rough but tolerable. We were allowed to keep our money, and could obtain additional food from town whenever the kitchen staff went into Sered proper to make daily camp purchases.

The camp baker, Mr. Heller, was a former pupil of my father and a member of his synagogue. On Sabbath eve he presented Mother with two small freshly baked *Hallahs,* and Father made *Kiddush* on them.

The apparent ease with which individuals could move about led my father to take Heller into his confidence. Mother was still perturbed about the absence of her woolen head scarf which she had left behind in the castle, and as she was complaining of a pain in her ear, it was decided to purchase a new scarf.

"I'll give Heller some money on Monday," Father comforted her. "He can buy you a scarf in town."

How soon this hope fell! At ten o'clock that Saturday morning we were all ordered to line up in the huge camp square and hand over all gold, silver, jewelry, furs, and money.

Gold and silver! What a cynical joke. The Jews of Slovakia had had their furs and jewels impounded against a "receipt" as far back as 1941. Only wedding rings were allowed to be retained. But Brunner was going to be "fair." He let it be known that no punishment would be meted out to anyone who had disobeyed the 1941 orders of the "silly Slovaks" and kept their gold, silver, furs, or jewelry, provided these valuables were now handed over to his S.S. men without question.

Father was worried about the new order, not because we had piles of gold and silver (actually we did not have any in 1941, with the exception of Mother's engagement ring), but because he was most reluctant to handle money on a Saturday.

"Perhaps it would be advisable to leave the money here in the barrack, and say that we haven't got any to hand over," he suggested.

"Impossible," I told him, aghast. "You must give them some-

[47]

thing. You cannot stand up before the S.S. men and declare you haven't a penny. They would never believe you."

"Indeed they wouldn't," Father agreed, perplexed. "Probably then, in circumstances such as these, we are permitted to handle money rather than involve ourselves in some danger. Brunner's temper must not be provoked. . . . The man is a maniac."

This compromise having been decided upon, we joined the huge single-line queue stretching like a snake over the vast compound. To our surprise, however, Brunner was nowhere to be seen. Rumors spread quickly: Brunner had escaped during the night; Brunner had been arrested for converting the confiscated jewelry of the previous transport to his own use, etc., etc. While we were relieved to see no sign of the hated face of Brunner, we were shocked at the sight of such a large number of new faces in the queue—Jewish men, women and children. It was obvious that Brunner's men dispersed all over the country were busy. Every few hours two or three newly captured victims were driven into Sered. The great hunt was on. No bunker was one hundred per cent safe. Eager anti-Semites curried favor with the Germans by reporting any suspicious movements in the houses of their neighbors who might be hiding Jewish families. One after the other they were hauled out of their secret bunkers.

My two older brothers, Julius and Alexander, went to England in 1939, and we were all happy with the knowledge that at least they were spared these terrible experiences; but our anxiety concerning the safety of my two sisters, Paula and Golda, and their families in Nitra grew with every moment. We knew they were hidden in a cellar in the out-of-town house of a customs and excise official. Once inside their cellar they were not allowed out under any circumstances, for milkmen, postmen, dustmen, delivery boys, meter-readers, charwomen, and even school children were encouraged by the Germans to report the sight of any "new faces" and to take note of any unusually large grocery order sent in to any of the shops. The Gestapo needed only the slightest clue; then they descended quickly and efficiently.

My sisters in their bunkers were living on the strictest rations. Only at night and during air raid alarms were they allowed out into the fresh air. When everyone else fled into the safety of air raid shelters the Jews ventured out into the open. Indeed, nothing made the evening seem more inviting and agreeable than the heavy drone of Allied bombers hovering overhead. At least it meant a short and fairly safe release from the dank, confined atmosphere of the bunkers.

In the huge queue on the camp grounds my heart sank as I recognized a number of familiar faces. There was Baruch Stern, our former neighbor, his attractive wife, Blanca, their three-month-old baby, and their four-year-old daughter, Mirike. Mirike was an exceptionally beautiful girl, whose huge black eyes, rosy cheeks, and lovely curls were yet to save her mother's life. Then there was Benzi and his family, and all other "*Amerikaner,*" as we were called. Also in the queue was Mrs. Gisi Fleischmann, that heroine of Slovakian Jewry, who in the height of the deportations in 1942 had the courage and initiative to offer Herr von Wisliczeni, the cursed German Adviser to the Slovakian government who initiated the deportations, a vast sum of money in return for the lives of the rest of Slovakia's Jews. Following a plan devised by that great and heroic leader, Rabbi M. D. Weissmandel (a son-in-law of my former teacher, the famous Rabbi S. D. Ungar, of Nitra), Mrs. Fleischmann, with a handful of others, placed a paper parcel containing fifty thousand dollars on Wisliczeni's desk, with a promise of more to follow, in return for stopping future transports to Auschwitz.

The bribe worked. For two long years the Jews of Slovakia lived in comparative safety, knowing that whatever happened they would not be deported. Then the blow fell which put an end to all hopes. When Wisliczeni's successor, Anton Brunner, arrived to take over, he made a deal with Mrs. Fleischmann, but on different terms. "Give me the addresses of all the Jews still hiding in the country," he said, "and I offer you absolute safety."

Gisi Fleischmann did not even answer him, and here she was now in the line, waiting to hand over her money and valuables with the rest of us.

The handing-over ceremony was a "peaceful" affair. There were no incidents and no questions.

"You may keep your watches and your wedding rings," came the gracious announcement. They wouldn't dream of taking these away from us—not yet, anyway.

If there was no trouble that morning, there was much fear and panic.

"It means deportation!" whispered the elder internees. "On the eve of every transportation from Sered they take away our money and valuables."

"But how is it possible?" we asked with faint optimism. "There are no more than 600 or 700 people in the queue this morning. That isn't enough for a transport."

By next morning, however, we found the answer to all our queries right on our doorstep, for there outside the camp gates, preceded by a joyous Brunner, shambled a long queue of Jews.

Brunner had "uncovered" the only Jewish old age home left in the country, a home whose safety had been guaranteed both by the Slovakian and the German authorities. And now they were all here!

Never before was there so much hatred and horror in the hearts of the Sered internees as at this very moment when these old and ailing people limped into the camp on their sticks, or were pushed in in wheel chairs, or were marched in on stretchers. The Jewish police were hurried towards the main entrance to carry the rucksacks and other belongings of the aged. Brunner had told the poor victims that they would be removed to "another" home. They had believed him until they noticed the wire fences and watchtowers. Then slowly and sadly came the dread disillusionment. This pitiful group of old people, about 150 of them, all over the age of seventy, tramped their way into the barrack next to ours, or were carried into it. Their groans and lamentations as they realized that the evening of their lives would end in the dark, hellish chambers of Auschwitz, were too much for my father. He loved and respected old people, and in all his years as rabbi had never missed his regular visits to the old age home in Bratislava to comfort and cheer them.

"I am going in to speak to them," he exclaimed.

"No, no!" I protested desperately. "All these days you have managed to hide your calling; now you want to reveal yourself in one unguarded moment. What good will it do them or you?"

Mother added her appeal to mine that Father should remain in our own room, but he would not heed us.

At the entrance of the barrack he stationed himself and bade each of the old people a hearty *Shalom Aleikhem* and asked them to listen quietly for a few moments.

"Some of you, my dear friends, may recognize me," he began. "I surely recognize many of you. But even if you don't know me, let me assure you that I am a Jew who has spent his entire life in the service of God and His *Torah*."

I trembled with anguish and fear. But the old people were hushed into silence. They always liked to listen to a sermon; they yearned for a word of comfort and reassurance, and longed for it now more than ever. They drew nearer to Father, straining their weak ears to make sure of hearing every word he said, and begged him to continue.

"Some irresponsible person," Father declared, "has spread

the rumor that we will all be deported from here. Let me assure you that there is not a word of truth in this. I have it on the highest authority that there will be no more transports from here."

"How can you know?" asked one of the assembled.

"Unfortunately, I am not allowed to disclose to you the source of this information. It is strictly confidential. But in order to reassure you of the correctness of my statement I give you my solemn word of honor, I swear to you by my *Olam Haba,* by my place in the world to come, by the dearest and most precious possession of a religious Jew, that what I have just told you is true and valid."

A deep sigh of relief was torn from the old people. One could almost hear a heavy burden falling from their frail shoulders. They believed Father. He had been able to inject some new hope and life into them. They settled down more easily and in a quieter mood.

When we returned to our room I reproached my father.

"How can you say such things? If anyone reports you to the guards, if anyone finds out that you are a rabbi, you will be in the gravest danger. And, in any case," I went on bitterly, "you know very well that we *are* going to Auschwitz . . . the number is growing every hour!"

"My son," Father answered gently. "You know that I was never one to take chances. It is not wise to run risks at a time of danger. But these poor and broken old people next door whose only wish and prayer is to die quietly and peacefully in their own beds, and to have a decent Jewish burial, needed a few words of encouragement and comfort more than anything else. Can't you see that their tragedy is a thousand times greater and sadder than ours? It was my duty to get up and offer them a ray of light and hope. And if, with God's help, I succeeded in making their fate a little easier to bear, then it is worth much more to me than the *Olam Haba* that I have staked on a false oath."

This may well have been the last lesson that I heard from my father's lips. It was most certainly his finest.

THE NIGHT of Tuesday, October 17, 1944, was one I shall never forget. It was filled with dreadful rumors, following a day of grave anxiety. We knew beyond any shadow of doubt that the next morning would see us herded into a transport. All the preparations, the strict security measures, the confinement of everyone to his barrack, the order to keep the rucksacks ready, the reinforcement of the camp guards, pointed only to one conclusion—deportation. All the bitter struggles of the past two and a half years, all the desperate efforts to save ourselves from deportation, all the changing hopes that in spite of all the odds we would manage somehow to survive the war without being separated, now faded away into a faint shadow.

But there were also wild and exciting rumors which spread in the camp as fast as a forest fire. During the day we heard that the Hungarian ruler, Admiral Horty, had asked the Russians for an armistice. In spite of the strict censorship, the news of this request and of the desertion of the Hungarian chief of staff to the Russians, announced on Budapest Radio, had reached Sered Camp. The Russians were thus only a hundred kilometers away from us, a distance which, with the collapse of opposition in Hungary, they could travel within four or five hours.

"Perhaps, with God's help, we might just make it," Mother said.

Would the Russians be in time to save the lives of a few hundred innocent Jews, or would they just miss us? These and a thousand other wild thoughts were with us all through this, our last night in Sered.

By the morning we awoke to the stark reality that there would be no Russians. Horty, the Hungarian dictator, had resigned and been replaced by a new man whose first act was to withdraw the request for an armistice. Brunner and his henchmen were all there, and so was an eighteen-truck train, standing bleakly empty on the camp siding.

As for us, we were all packed, our rucksacks bulging with all sorts of food and clothing. It was the first day of the Jewish month *Heshvan,* and while I stood consumed by fear, Father in his *Tallit* and *Tefillin,* recited the usual morning prayers, plus the Additional Service of the New Month. We were in no mood for breakfast—the atmosphere was too tense and panicky. Then we paused to hear an announcement that everyone should line up outside his barrack ready for further transportation.

"Mixed married couples, children of such marriages, and others who consider that they have good reason to be excluded from the transport," came the announcement, "must wait in the toilet until they are called for an interview."

"We had better go there," Father suggested, "and try and talk ourselves out of deportation. It is our only chance."

"But what shall we say?" Mother asked nervously. "Surely you will not say that one of us is . . ."

"God forbid," said Father hastily. "My idea is to show

[55]

Brunner the letter from the Palestine office in Budapest, confirming that a certificate of entry into Palestine awaits us there, should we be able to make the journey."

"But will he accept it?" Mother went on.

"Mammele," said Father affectionately, "we must try to make use of even the most slender chance. If it be God's will, we might succeed."

Father then suggested that Mother, who could speak Brunner's Viennese German, should be the spokesman. She agreed.

As Brunner opened the toilet door he was met by quite a crowd. First there was that woman from the castle who had claimed that her American passport was with the police in Topolcany. She asked Brunner whether he had taken any steps to collect it.

"*Ja, ja,*" Brunner waved her away. "We will get your passport for you. In the meantime you must join the queue outside." He finished with her quickly. Not so with the next victim.

"Ah," said Brunner as a man flung himself to attention before him. "I know you. You are Haar, the fellow who tried to hide in the castle. What do you want?"

"*Herr Hauptsturmfuehrer,*" said Haar in a firm voice. "My wife is an Aryan."

"Where is she?"

"In the hospital in Banska Bistrica."

Brunner knew that Banska Bistrica was in the hands of the partisans, and that he could not, therefore, check on Haar's statement.

"Get into the line," he ordered.

"But *Herr Hauptsturmfuehrer,*" Haar appealed, "my wife *is* an Aryan."

"Liar!" snapped Brunner. But for some reason he was not in his usual bad temper, and Haar sensed it. He came to attention again, and appealed once more.

"Okay," Brunner said, "you join the mixed marriage quarters."

"Thank you, *Herr Hauptsturmfuehrer*," said Haar gratefully, and disappeared behind the barrack.

Brunner turned to us with a cynical grin.

"And who is the Aryan in your lot?" he asked as Mother approached him with a piece of paper in her trembling hands. She curtsied before him as though he were royalty. Poor Mummy, she played her part so well as she appealed to him in true Viennese slang:

"*Ich bitte Herr Hauptschaarfuehrer um Gnade . . .* I beg you, *Herr Hauptschaarfuehrer* for mercy and for recognition of this document."

In her excitement she mixed up his rank, and handed the letter to him. He gave it a momentary glance, enough to see the title, and then burst into a yell: "For mercy you apply to the Pope, and as for the document . . . These cursed Zionists: they want you in Palestine . . . Well, you won't get there . . . never, never, never . . ."

Mother was as white as a ghost as, trembling wildly, she finished her ordeal.

"Don't worry, Mammele," said Father gently. "I never really expected him to be hoodwinked. I just wanted to try it for our own satisfaction. At least we know we have tried our best."

By the time we joined the long queue of rucksack-bearing, Auschwitz-bound Jews, it was almost midday. Although it was mid-October, the sun shone down bright and warm, as if making a special effort to comfort us with its warm and soothing rays. From the distance we watched the Jewish police loading the first three wagons with the old people from Nove Mesto. One by one they were lifted into the cattle trucks, and set down on the floor like bales of wheat or flour. It was a dreadful sight. I heard Father murmur: "Oh, Almighty God!

Perhaps we don't deserve any better; but these old people . . . Please be merciful upon them; make it easy for them."

Special guards were mounted all over the camp. Those who were allowed to stay on were confined to their barracks. Sered was as quiet as a cemetery as it made ready to take leave of another eight hundred victims. Yes, Brunner had somehow managed to get together eight hundred Jews, and he was not prepared to risk losing any by a few days' waiting. He paraded along the line in full battle dress, armed to the teeth, and flanked by two S.S. men carrying Bren-guns. What a coward *Hauptsturmfuehrer* Anton Brunner was! Whenever there was a transport leaving, so they said in Sered, he would not dare move about without his revolver, and an armed escort. The cold, cynical murderer was afraid of his own shadow, afraid of the revenge that might come from aged and infirm people. . . .

The panic among the transport was indescribable. A number of internees, particularly women, ran back into the barracks to relieve themselves, for excitement and fear had brought forth their natural reactions. Ruthless S.S. men beat them out of the toilets with their revolvers and rifle butts; children screamed, women wept, and the men had to stand by helplessly.

Internees from each barrack in the camp were marched out to the train separately. The Jewish police marched them as far as the gates, and from there the S.S., with their well-tried system of abuse, threats, and speed-up, took over.

On the sidings the sliding doors of the cattle wagons were pushed wide open, a wooden ramp was pushed against the door, and the victims had to run up and into the wagon. The S.S. men were drunk with a new excess of hate. They yelled, pushed, knocked down, and kicked everyone who was not moving fast enough. Nobody was spared. Even women carrying their babies in their arms, and with a heavy rucksack tied to their shoulders, were helped along with a jackboot or a rifle butt.

Once inside, we were all overcome by the heavy smell of cattle-dung. Everyone rushed to the walls; everyone searched for at least a little comfort, and for something to lean against. Within seconds the walls were flanked, mostly by youngsters, while the slower-moving elders found themselves stranded in the middle of the wagon. Immediately, Father took the initiative.

"Mr. Gottlieb," he said to Benzi, "I want you to take charge of this wagon, and I am asking everyone to obey orders. Even if the S.S. behave like beasts, even if we are treated like animals, that doesn't mean that we should behave as such! On the contrary, we must keep ourselves respectable and orderly."

Benzi set to work immediately. Younger people were removed from the sides of the wagon, and women and elderly people placed against them; small children were set on their mothers' laps. The rest of us gathered in the middle. As the S.S. men pushed shut the doors, a dirty bucket was flung in, and then the wagon was sealed.

It was pitch-dark for a few moments. The two little airing windows were heavily barred with wire, and with fifty people in each wagon, and no room for the rucksacks, the air became thick and nauseating.

Suddenly the doors were opened again. Outside stood that woman from the Castle again arguing with an S.S. man about her American passport which was supposed to be with the police in Topolcany. Brunner came along. He recognized her immediately.

"Karl," he shouted to the S.S. man, "this 'lady'"—again the stress on the word *lady*—"this lady gets out at Topolcany. She's an American . . . a citizen of the United States of America."

The woman was pushed into our wagon. She tried to turn

round and thank Brunner for his kindness, but the doors clanged shut behind her.

At four o'clock there came a shrill blast from a whistle, the engine gave a strong pull, and the wheels rumbled into a devil's tattoo.

The dreaded, unspeakable journey to infamous Auschwitz had begun. . . .

II AUSCHWITZ

SLOWLY THE train puffed its way out of the bleak siding as if it knew the horror to which it was bearing its human load. Even the wild shooting of the trigger-happy killers to celebrate our departure was less frightening than that slow reluctance of the engine to move.

Inside the wagon a deathly silence had descended. Everyone sat or stood quietly and motionless in his cramped place. Even an eight-month-old baby—the first-born of a couple who had been childless for twelve years—slept quietly on her mother's lap, worn out with the endless movement, agitation, and unceasing noise of that cruel day.

Most of the people in our wagon, I observed, were Bratislavians. I recognized skinny Mr. Federweiss, an insurance agent, with his wife and two children; Bibi Stern, a well-known figure in Bratislava, and his family; the Rosenbergs, once rich cattle-dealers and well-known communal workers at home. How could they have dreamed that their own days would come to an end by a journey in the cattle train that had borne so many of their livestock to the market? Mrs. Rosen-

[63]

berg had tried to present herself as an Aryan before the transport set off. Brunner had eyed her for a few minutes—she was a very attractive woman—and then he had said:

"Recite to me the prayer, *Vater Unser!*"

She began in a shaky voice:

"Our Father, which art in heaven, Hallowed be Thy Name. Thy kingdom come. Thy will be done, on earth as it is in heaven. Give us this day our daily bread. And forgive us our trespasses, as we forgive them that trespass against us. And lead us not into temptation; But deliver us from evil. Amen."

When she had finished, Brunner pushed her into the queue.

The wagon was rocking now as the engine got up speed. Above the rhythm of the heavy wheels came a shrill voice piercing our deadened senses.

"We are not going to Auschwitz, after all. We are going to Austria!"

Hope.

Strange how quickly and enthusiastically doomed people will grasp even the most slender chance of survival. But optimism is a drug without which one could not possibly survive in circumstances such as we were facing, and as a drug, it worked quickly.

"That's right," came another excited voice. "There is a new camp in Austria, it is near Vienna, the work is easier. Families are allowed to remain together. There are no gas chambers there."

The tragic faces brightened: here was unhoped-for good news—but alas! not for long was it to hold.

"We shall soon see," said a third voice, eager to explain. "If the train turns right at Leopoldov junction, then, indeed, we shall be going to Austria via Bratislava. But if it turns left, then it is the way to Poland . . . and Auschwitz."

Everyone was holding his breath as the train rattled over the numerous crossings at Leopoldov. Bibi Stern, standing at the barred window, watched carefully the movements of the engine in front. His voice, shadowed with disillusion, struck down our every hope. "We are turning left!" he said slowly.

Before his words had died away, there came groans, cries, and lamentations which filled the wagon. As they grew in intensity my father stood silently reciting the Evening Prayers. Benzi stood up and raised his hands.

"Come on, boys and girls," he cried, motioning to them with his hands like a choirmaster. "Let us sing a few songs."

Without waiting he began to sing in his own strong and deep voice the last *Avinu Malkenu* from the Holy Days' Prayers. Slowly one youngster after the other joined him.

"Our Father and our King, be gracious unto us, and answer us: for though we are destitute of good works, yet act charitably and graciously with us, and save us."

This prayer, with its affecting melody, was never as apt and as moving as at that very moment. Again and again we sang it, more and more joined in, louder and louder became our prayer, until it almost deadened the noise of the rolling wheels.

This song must have put some courage into young Federweiss, for he edged his way to Father. "Rabbi," he said, "do you think I should use these?" He produced from his pockets a thin saw, a hammer, and a chisel.

"My dear Federweiss," Father began, but was interrupted by Mrs. Federweiss.

"Please, Rabbi," she implored, "don't let him use them. I begged him for weeks already to get rid of them. He bought a complete set of tools on the day the Germans occupied the country, and he is determined to break out and jump from the train. He wants me and the children to jump, too. How can my poor little children jump from a fast-moving train?" The poor woman broke into heart-rending sobs.

Young Federweiss and his wife were evidently looking to

[65]

Father as the one and only man who could give them the right answer.

"How can I advise you on so difficult a question?" Father said. "There is just no answer. You will have to decide this between yourselves."

Federweiss was not to be constrained. He pushed his way towards the offside of the wagon and began to work feverishly. His hammer attacked the chisel furiously. Then he sawed wildly at the first of the three hinges until it broke loose. Spurred on by this success he went on to the second hinge. Then a sharp pull on the engine brakes flung him to the floor and broke his saw in two, leaving one half stuck in the door. The train was brought to an unexpected stop at a small station. Federweiss's attempt to escape had failed for all time.

Peering into the windows of a passenger train standing on the opposite platform, I saw a reflection of our train. The S.S. occupied the first, middle, and last coaches—passenger compartments, of course—and now they were alighting quickly and patrolling the platform. On the other platform I saw a man, accompanied by his young wife, hurrying to the waiting train. He jumped in, lowered the window of his compartment, and bent forward to kiss her good-bye. Soon his train moved out of the platform and I heard him calling happily to her: "See you tomorrow, dear!"

As our train lurched forward I left the window and sat down sadly in our dark wagon. A million questions stormed my mind. "See you tomorrow, dear!" I repeated to myself, apparently louder than I intended to.

"What are you saying?" asked Father.

"I am talking about that happy man in that other train!" I shot out. "That lucky fellow who is fortunate enough to have been born a non-Jew. . . . Because of this, he will be back home tomorrow, in his own home, with his own wife, sleeping in his own bed."

Father turned reproachful eyes on me.

"You mustn't talk like this," he said gently. "We must not lose faith. We must be strong and brave, now more so than ever."

"But tell me why," I cut in. The train incident I had just witnessed had shaken my lifelong belief. I was so desperate I could not bear Father's quiet and unshaken trust in God. The little baby on her mother's lap woke up at that very moment and began to cry for her milk.

"Milky, Mummy. . . . Milky," she begged piteously. Her mother tried to push a bottle between her open lips, but the child pushed it out. It did not want a cold bottle; it wanted a warm drink. The mother unbuttoned her cardigan and I watched her push the bottle between her breasts in an effort to warm it up a little. My mother saw it, too, and began to weep quietly.

"Mammele," Father turned to her. "Don't upset yourself. You must keep strong. It is God's will that we be here today. It will surely turn out for the best."

"But how? Oh, Almighty God, how? And how could Ilonka and her children have survived this journey?" Mother burst out. "Can't you hear *her* own little children crying for a warm drink?"

Father tried desperately to quiet her, for following Mother's example, others in the wagon began to cry too. Father had to stop her before panic broke out.

Fortunately there was another distraction. The train slowed down again at the approach of another station. The woman from the castle who had left her passport with the police at Topolcany, jumped from her seat and rushed wildly to the door. She trod on people and rucksacks alike, and hammered her fists madly against the sealed doors.

"This is Topolcany," she yelled. "Let me out; I want my passport. Let me out!"

[67]

The poor woman, who had put her trust in the cynical Brunner, and indeed expected that he would allow her to alight at Topolcany to fetch her American passport, went mad as the train whistled its way past the station. Blood trickled from her hands as she hammered her fists frantically against the ironclad doors.

On Father's instructions, Benzi and I gently pulled her away from the door. She kicked and pleaded: "I *am* an American; my passport is genuine. I don't belong here. . . . Let me out." Seeing the hopelessness of her plight, she collapsed on her rucksack. Benzi put a flask of brandy to her lips, but though she recovered, she never opened her eyes again during the journey.

The train lumbered on, struggling its way up the Carpathian mountain track, until we eventually lapsed into an uneasy semiconsciousness which was not deep enough for slumber. Benzi spent the best part of the night passing the dirty bucket around, and emptying it every so often through a small gap between the doors and the edge of the wagon—a thankless task, but a necessary one, which he performed with magnificent selflessness.

At dawn the forlorn baby's cry for "milky" brought me to my feet again. The air was cool, and in spite of the stuffy atmosphere in the wagon, I felt chilled to the bone. Carefully, I tiptoed my way to the window and waited until we passed a station again. I had not long to wait. We approached one. Would the train stop? No. But as we passed through I noticed that the railwayman's uniform was strange to me, and so was the name of the station. *We were in Poland!* We had crossed the border; we had been smuggled out of the country of our birth without passport or visa. The sun was fighting its way up from the horizon. The train rolled faster and faster; the poor baby fell asleep again as I made my way back to Father.

"We are in Poland," I said.

"Shush!" Father hushed me, pointing to Mother who was sleeping crumpled up on her rucksack. "Don't tell anybody!" he whispered.

"It is time to put your *Tefillin* on for *Shaharit*," Father said quietly as he prepared for Morning Service. He put on his *Tefillin*. I put on mine, and he stood quietly, fervent prayers on his lips. Tears welled in his eyes as he began to recite the *Hallel* Prayer to mark the second day of *Rosh Hodesh Heshvan*.

Did he know? Did he know that this was to be the very last Morning Prayer in his life? Did he know that this was the very last *Hallel* he would recite in this world? Was that the answer to his tears?

He must have known! He must have felt that his prayer, *Ono Hashem Hoshio No* — Please O Lord, Help!—would this time remain unanswered.

He must have known all this and yet tried desperately to hide his feelings. He turned to me, as he always did, saying: "Please, son, pray slowly and with devotion. It is *Rosh Hodesh* today."

The morning hours dragged on. Benzi tried to start a singsong again, but there was no response. Benzi did not try again. He was too exhausted and too dispirited to set us going a second time. Besides, his two young children were growing restless, and his wife was eaten up with anxiety. I made my way to the window again. We were still miles from nowhere, the train going at top speed, when suddenly I burst out:

"Here! A dugout, with an S.S. man in it."

There was a mad rush for the little window. Every few minutes we passed a little dugout in the open field, occupied by an S.S. man in full battle dress manning a mounted machine gun and watching our train through field glasses.

"We must be near the Russian front," came someone's voice from the back. "Perhaps the train driver is a partisan, and is taking us all to the Russians?"

Hope dies hard.

"Perhaps indeed he is," echoed Federweiss. "For what other reason could these S.S. men be out here in the open?"

Yes, we thought of everything except the ominous truth. Who would have dreamed that some twenty kilometers away from the infamous extermination camp there would already be S.S. outposts ready to shoot down any escapees? Who in his wildest imagination could have pictured Auschwitz to be what it actually was—a place that was Hell itself.

But we had not gotten there yet. The train went on and on; the outposts became more and more frequent until finally we saw the camp in the distance. What a vast beehive! . . . what a jungle of filthy dog-houses! . . . what an inferno! . . . horrible . . . frightening . . . a huge cage to trap the living Jew, and then destroy him until there was nothing left except crumbling, charred bones. Has history ever thrown up, in its thousands of years, such bestial, satanic death mills?

The sprawling vastness of Auschwitz as seen from a fast-moving train was indescribable. For miles and miles the speeding train showed us nothing but barracks, watchtowers, barbed wire entanglements, S.S. dugouts, guards with Alsatian dogs, and a veritable phalanx of thousands upon thousands of what looked to be old and ragged people. But the Germans were shrewd. They tried to dissemble the true picture of the abysmal filth of Auschwitz for as long as they possibly could. Part of this sadistic game of deception was the number of tidy-looking barracks along the railway route where one could see diapers and baby clothing hanging on the washing lines. Perambulators and cots stood serenely outside block entrances. We were all fooled . . . for a time.

Father eagerly called Mother to the window.

"You see," he called reassuringly, "there are babies and small children in this camp. Look at all these diapers and prams, look at all these old people, look at their old clothing: they must have been here for years and years. You see it proves that people *do* live in Auschwitz."

Mother was not deceived, but Father continued to try to reassure her.

"We'll manage to survive all this," he added confidently. "After all, the Russians can't be too far away. It is a matter of weeks. With God's help we shall be with Ilonka and the children by tonight."

Yes, and indeed they were . . . but not the way Father had meant it.

1

IT WAS exactly eleven A.M. when the train jerked to a stop.

"*Raus, Raus!*", shouted a thousand voices, as the wagon doors were torn ajar. The shouts were deafening. S.S. men with whips and half-wild Alsatian dogs swarmed all over the place. Uncontrolled fear brought panic as families were ruthlessly torn apart. Parents screamed for lost children and mothers shrieked their names over the voices of the bawling guards. Everyone without exception lost both nerves and senses—and this played right into the hands of the S.S. men. They had set out to break our morale, to wipe away every trace of human feeling, to drive fear, dread, and panic into us. The spine-chilling terror infused in us at the very moment of our arrival never left us. It was all part of Himmler's plan to help along his extermination policy. All possibilities of revolt were to be stamped out before ever we entered the Cage of Death.

"Leave everything in the wagon," the S.S. men ordered. "It will all be brought to your barracks later. *Raus*—quickly! Line up five deep. *Raus! Raus! Raus.*"

There was a bustle in our wagon. Two burly S.S. men tried

to grab a mother and her son as they sat motionless on the floor. But they were too late. The young chemist and his widowed mother were not prepared to let Auschwitz gas them with cyanide, and then use their bones to make phosphates, and extract their fat to make soap. Instead, they swallowed the cyanide, hidden in a slice of salami, and died instantly. The S.S. men were furious.

"Cursed cowards!" yelled one at the top of his voice. "Afraid of an honest day's work . . . *Verfluchte Feiglinge!*"

The fact that two harmless people had cheated them by preferring death to delivering themselves into their murderous hands, drove the S.S. to even greater fury and temper. With clenched fists and upraised rifle butts they cleared everybody out of the wagon. In a matter of seconds the whole train was empty.

The poor victims still clung to their few paltry belongings. In spite of the S.S. threats, in spite of all the pushing and kicking, in spite of the command for speed, each grabbed hold of his or her rucksack or handbag, and ran for the queue.

Suddenly a line of Auschwitz inmates, dressed in their striped prison-type uniforms, arrived at the train side. They were called "*Canadians*" or "*Kanadians*" for reasons unknown to us at the time. Their job was to unload the luggage from the train into waiting army lorries. They were all Jews, but were not allowed to speak to any of us. Later, we learned that "*Kanada*" was a nickname given to a certain area of the great death camp by prisoners, in which thirty-five warehouses packed with clothing and other articles, including glasses, artificial limbs and women's hair, provided grim material for the Auschwitz death industries—that terrifying factory organized by I. G. Farben. At one time three thousand privileged prisoners were engaged sorting out this spoliation of the Jews' personal property.

My parents and I, each with our rucksacks, quickly joined

the queue of the doomed, flanked by wildly barking Alsatian dogs and their bloodthirsty handlers. Horrible odors—the strong disinfectant which pervaded the camp; the smell of burning hair and roasting human flesh emanating from the four vast crematoria and the forty-six ovens, ovens with a capacity for burning twelve thousand bodies every twenty-four hours—the pestilential smells of Auschwitz—seeped into us, making us retch and gasp for a breath of unpolluted air.

"Old people, or anyone too tired to march, should sit down here. They will be collected in lorries," screamed the S.S. men, as they ordered everyone else in line. The old people from the Nove Mesto old age home, those poor elders of Slovakian Jewry, sat down on the cold platform in gratitude, grabbing hold of the rucksacks containing their small but very precious possessions. Little did they know they would be exterminated the moment they entered Auschwitz. Himmler had no use for feeble prisoners.

"That's right," said those ferocious sons of Hitler's master race. "You sit yourselves down nicely, and we will soon have you fetched and taken to your 'rooms.'"

"Thank you," said the poor, deluded old folks as they explained that the journey had been hard for them, and apologized for not being able to march along with the rest of the queue.

By now the children were panic-stricken as, without a word from anyone, men, women, and children were marched into the camp in rows five deep. When we came to within shouting distance of the prisoners behind the barbed wire, we realized that they were all young people—very young indeed—who looked old because of their shabby clothing, starved faces, and clean-shaven heads.

"Where are we?" some called out to them. "What is going to happen to us? Is there anything we ought to know."

There was no answer from the debilitated prisoners. Their

lips remained sealed as they watched us with their dead eyes joining the legions of the condemned. A few of them looked greedily at our cigarettes, the most precious currency in the camp, but that we did not understand. Our eyes were darting here, there, and everywhere. We could not see quickly enough. Gate after gate was opened and clanged shut behind us; everywhere we were counted. Those who faltered on the march were again invited to "stay behind." Always a few dropped out, thinking that there was at least a grain of mercy in their captors. They would be gassed for their pains.

On we marched, past a hundred warning signs reading: "Beware! High Tension Wire!" Each of these signs had the S.S. symbol and the emblem of skull and crossbones. Then we marched past huge pits filled with charred bones where, whenever the crematoria could not cope with the number of gassed prisoners, the bodies were dumped, soaked in petrol, and set alight. Who could now doubt we were in Auschwitz? Who could now doubt it, as we marched past hundreds of watchtowers, with their trigger-happy guards and mounted machine guns ready to fire at the least provocation . . . or without it?

On we marched and marched . . . marching into the city of the doomed and the hell that Himmler had prepared for us with such scientific thoroughness. How could the rest of the world stand aloof while this, the greatest tragedy, the greatest horror, that ever tortured mankind, grew in intensity day by day?

      ✿   ✿   ✿   ✿   ✿   ✿   ✿

The actual section of the camp we arrived at was Birkenau. It used to be, and indeed looked like, a rest-place for sick horses of the Polish army. On many of the barracks remained the original notices giving instructions for the treatment of infected animals. There were three main sections to this concentration city: Auschwitz I, Auschwitz II (Birkenau), and Auschwitz III (Monowitz).

Auschwitz II, or Birkenau, was, to all intents and purposes, a separate camp, consisting mainly of wooden huts and barracks, whereas Auschwitz I had several stone barracks and brick buildings. But there was no difference in the evil that pervaded them both.

As we were shepherded deeper and deeper into camp, past zigzag crossings and behind more and more clanging gates, there came into sight a small square red-brick building. From its short chimney shot out tongues of bright flame.

Benzi's little boy, Harry, turned to his father. "Daddy," he asked, "what is this house? There is fire coming from the chimney."

"Must be a laundry," said Benzi thickly, patting his child's pale cheeks with his plump fingers. "Yes, it is a laundry, and the stoker must have put too much wood on the fire."

Mother and I, like everyone else in that line of the doomed, had our eyes turned to that strange, dreadful building. Our thoughts were controlled, but not our fears. Father alone refused to look at the furnace. He kept his eyes fixed on us and said, with a brave show of utter calm: "Yes, it is a laundry. They have such small brick laundries here in Poland. They believe that the shorter the chimney, the less fuel is needed for the fire."

Father always had a reasonable answer ready, valid and acceptable. His motive, no doubt, was to calm, since no one could now be reassured. We were too near the end of our earthly lives.

The building passed from our view—the first of Auschwitz's four huge crematoria—but the ghastly miasma followed us along our half-hour's march to the halt outside a barrack.

We were let in one by one through a small door so that the S.S. men could count us, and as we passed out of the daylight we were ordered to occupy the right or left side of the barrack, leaving the center passage free for the two dozen S.S. men outside.

Mother was pale and tired from exhaustion and almost fell down on her rucksack, but Father showed no sign of strain as he pulled out two sandwiches from his coat pocket and bade us eat them. I wanted no food.

"But you must eat," he urged. "You never know how long it will be before we get settled in our barrack. You'd better eat now, while we have this little break."

He put a sandwich in my hand and as I nibbled at it I surveyed the barrack and the people in it.

A hollow brick ledge, used for heating, ran down the center of the block from one end to the other, leading to the chimney. This ledge separated the prisoners into two sections, enabling the S.S. walking along the brickwork to survey their victims on both sides. Around us, a thick gray hose surrounded the entire barrack.

"We will be gassed in here," whispered Baruch Stern, my former neighbor, to Benzi.

"Don't be ridiculous," answered Benzi. "Can't you see the holes round the walls? The gas would escape in no time."

For men discussing their probable end, such details may seem frivolous, but in dire emergencies men catch upon the slightest diversion.

A few inmates—*Haeftlinge,* as they were called—mingled among us. They were all members of the *Kanada* group. One had his eyes fixed on Stern's little daughter, Mirike, that beautiful little girl with the piercing black eyes and huge long curls. He went across to Baruch's wife, Blanca.

"Are you the mother of this little girl?" he whispered.

"Yes."

"Then move away from her. . . . Mix with the unmarried

girls. Maybe one day you will get the chance to have more such lovely little girls."

"What do you mean?" asked the bewildered mother, as she held Mirike by the hand, and tightened her hold on the pram in which lay her few-months'-old baby.

The question was never answered, for at that moment the door of the barrack was flung open and at the shout of *Achtung* a column of S.S. men filed in. The *Kanadian* moved away from Blanca.

At the head of the S.S. stood Dr. Mengele, the high-ranking S.S. doctor, who was in charge of the "selections." The dreaded moment had arrived. My tongue clove to the roof of my mouth.

At first an S.S. man stood on a chair and began to read off some names from a list. Among the first was that of Mrs. Gisi Fleischmann, who had saved many of her brethren from the very situation in which she now found herself. She answered her name and was led out. She was never seen again.

The bestial work of extermination had already begun. "Selection" was a simple but scientific principle. Those who were too weak to work, or were considered especially dangerous, died that day; others were retained for certain duties. But life expectancy in Auschwitz was no longer than three months, even for the *Kanadians*.

Suddenly Dr. Mengele put a stop to the name-reading and marched along the brick chimney, holding his right hand between his jacket buttons and directing operations with his left thumb. He stared at each one of us, and if he gave a turn of the thumb, it meant that the person so indicated should step out. He told everyone who was over forty-five to remain where he was. *"Dort bleiben; dort bleiben!"* he would say calmly to anyone trying to step out without being called.

I summed up the situation in one second.

"Papa," I said desperately. "You can easily say you are under forty-five and come with me. You see what's happening?"

"How can I leave Mummy here alone?" he said reproachfully. "How can I let her carry our rucksacks alone into the barracks for us?"

Into our discussion came an interruption. An old man sidled up to Father. His name was Zodek Haar, an old Bratislavian, who although in the group of the Nove Mesto aged people, insisted on marching along with the rest of us, rather than be "picked up" by lorries.

"Well, Rabbi," he said to Father. "And what do you have to tell me now?" He was obviously referring to Father's reassuring little speech way back at Sered.

"I have to tell you," answered Father seriously, "that it is our duty to declare that we are prepared to submit to God's will, whatever it may be."

Desperate scenes were developing in the barrack, amounting to pandemonium. Heartbroken parents clamored to join their "selected" children; young children wanted to hold on to their "selected" fathers. The chaos was indescribable. S.S. men, determined to restore order, set about the concourse, beating and pounding them with their rifle butts. There were heartbreaking screams and cries, but the shrieks imbued the S.S. men with more fury. They hammered their rifles indiscriminately over the heads of their victims, they lashed out wildly right and left. Within seconds, unconscious, bleeding bodies lay all over the place. Parents, their faces smothered in blood, still screamed and searched for their children who had been lost in the mad welter of attack.

Dr. Mengele went on with his job unperturbed. He did not even move his right hand out of its rest between the jacket buttons. These were everyday scenes for him; they left him unmoved, perhaps a little bored. He kept on staring at every face. Nearer and nearer he came to us.

"Papa," I tried again, desperately. "You can . . . "

Father looked at Mother as she stood shivering in the line.

She was, and looked, older than he. Mother gave me a long gentle look, and my desperation fled. I no longer wanted to drag Papa away from her.

"Mamma," I breathed, and felt an overwhelming desire to go over to her for just one final second, to give one last little hug and kiss to that frightened and shaking, frail little woman who was my nearest and dearest, my most precious on earth, my own sweet and dear Mamma. Just for one second. But no!

"*Du*," came a wild command from the center of the barrack. "You there!" Mengele shouted at me. I swung round and he gave a glance at me. "Forward!" he said, motioning me with his left thumb. Immediately an S.S. grabbed hold of me and pulled me away. There was not even a ghost of a chance to turn round again; not even a short second to kiss Father's smooth and gentle hand; not even a second to say good-bye. Out, out they pushed me into the little annex adjoining the block.

"*Dort bleiben!*" I heard Dr. Mengele shout in the direction of Papa and Mamma. "*Dort bleiben!*"

There they remained and I had lost them . . . lost them forever.

Then my brain refused to work. It was a mercy. . . .

8

OUTSIDE IN that little wooden annex, I was still dazed, so much so that I had no will to think of the terrible tragedy that had just befallen me, or of the fate of my dearest parents from whom I had been brutally wrenched. For the first time in my life I found myself completely and irrevocably alone. Never before had I felt so lost and so terribly afraid. Then realization of our own doom returned. I searched desperately in the crowd of unhappy men, a crowd of fathers just torn away mercilessly from their young children, a crowd of husbands ripped cruelly from their wives, a crowd of youngsters pulled from their parents. They had no eyes for me. I stood forlorn and in utter despair in a crowd of forlorn and unseeing men, each hardly able to cope with his own tumultuous thoughts.

Then I saw Benzi and Baruch Stern coming out of the selection ordeal. Both of them had left their wives and children behind. Both of them were shaken and dazed; both, without words. But how glad I was to see them again. I hurried over to Baruch who was in tears.

"We'd better say our last prayers. I think we're all going to the gas chambers," he said in a faint voice.

His very despair heartened me. "I don't know about us," I forced myself to say. "But those next door are surely meant for it." My voice dried up. The thought was too cruel, too impossible. How could I make away with innocent and harmless strangers, even in my mind?

"We are all doomed," Baruch moaned. "They usually make the selections at the station. The fact that we were brought inside in one group means instant death for us all!"

"But why did they make the selection?" Benzi argued, trying to force hope into his own mind as well as ours.

"Perhaps they are afraid of having such a large group of young men present when their families are gassed—it is safer to separate us from them," ventured Baruch.

That explanation sounded so reasonable that we turned towards the wall and recited our last prayer. But no words would come from me. How could I, a nineteen-year-old youth, know what prayers to recite before departing this world? Where should I start? What should I say?

I just closed my eyes and kept on repeating the *Shema Yisroel*—Hear O Israel the Lord our God the Lord is One—over and over again. And as I prayed I was conscious that more and more people kept coming in from the barrack next door. I prayed harder, hoping, hoping that they would send my father out. I still had a forlorn hope that we would all be saved from this terrible and unbelievable nightmare.

But Dr. Mengele had concluded his "medical inspection." The last few people trickled into our annex until finally all the S.S. came out and the door was shut, bolted, and barred.

"Good-bye!" I murmured, and raised my arms longingly in the direction of the main barrack where I had left my dear parents. There was no time now for thoughts of anyone but myself.

"*Raus von hier!*" came the shouts and yells again. Out we were pushed into the open and lined up five deep. We were marched towards a white stone building some distance away, and brought to a halt outside the entrance.

In search of a cigarette, I found my half of the sandwich which Father had given me earlier. His words came back to me in a ghostly echo: "Eat the sandwich, my son. You might not have a chance later." I ate it. I could hardly swallow and it almost choked me, and all the time I kept my eye on this white stone building which looked so quiet and so strange. There were no windows in it. It could only be one thing—yes, it was—the gas chambers at last.

I glanced at my watch. The time was three o'clock, four hours since our arrival. In the distance the women who had been separated from the men immediately after "selection" were being marched away. Also, in the distance I noted with horror three army lorries laden with prams. There were cries and groans in our column as fathers recognized the empty prams of their precious babies. Then I saw a woman waving desperately towards us.

"Look!" I said to Baruch. "Look! I am sure that is Blanca waving to you from the line."

"Yes," he cried despairingly. "It looks like Blanca!—But how is it possible? Where is my Mirike? Where is my baby?"

It was Blanca all right, but these questions about his children remained his ever-present torment until after liberation, when Blanca, returning safely from the camp, told him that the *Kanadian* who had warned her in the barrack, grabbed her away from her children, pushed her in front of Dr. Mengele, and had her selected together with other girls. "If you stay here," the *Kanadian* told her, "you will never have another beautiful little girl like her—but if you go now, then you may perhaps have another chance."

There was so much that is even now incomprehensible.

Suddenly a group of S.S. broke upon us with strident shouts.

"Anyone unfit for hard labor . . . men with weak hearts or lung ailments . . . step aside for light work."

A few poor innocent fellows, seeing what they thought was a chance of redemption, stepped aside for "light work." They were marched off, never to be seen again.

With the departure of the duped victims, the doors of the white stone building were thrown open and we were forced inside.

It was a huge empty hall, with a few inmates in white and blue striped prison suits standing idly near the walls. S.S. men came in with us, ordering our group—about two hundred strong—to undress completely and put our clothing "nicely and tidily" on the floor so that we could find "everything in its place."

This done, we were ordered to form a single line round the hall.

"You may keep your shoes, glasses, and belts!" they bawled.

Then, like peddlers collecting pennies from a queue outside a cinema, the inmates or *Haeftlinge*, marched along the line of naked men with their caps in hand to collect watches, rings, and anything else that was of any value. My new watch went with the rest.

Finally, the S.S. stationed themselves in the center of the hall and every victim, shoes in hand, had to appear before them, hands and legs stretched wide apart and mouth open for inspection against smuggling. Again these S.S. men made yet another selection from the crowd of naked men. They examined our buttocks, for lean buttocks are a telltale of physical condition. "Step aside," they ordered those whom they considered unfit for heavy work.

From there we were taken, or, rather, shoved and beaten, into an adjoining room—the barbers' room.

It was the first and foremost rule of the sadistic tyranny that

[84]

whenever victims were to be moved from place to place, this was to be accompanied by constant yelling, beating, and thrashing—the same method that is used to herd and push along cattle. These bestial S.S. men hit and lashed out left and right into the mass of panic-stricken, naked victims without care or mercy.

"*Los . . . los!*" they yelled and hit. "Get going. Quicker! Faster! Quicker."

Everyone rushed towards the little door, trying desperately to get out of reach of the flailing S.S. and their stinging whips. Every few seconds the door was blocked by three or four people who tried to get through at the same time. The S.S. man, standing at the other side of the door, poked his rifle butt into their faces and stomachs, pushing them backwards. The terror was absolute.

Finally, we got through and found ourselves in an equally large hall lined on all sides with barbers—all inmates—each having a little chair in front of him. The S.S., who followed us, pushed us into these chairs and the barbers cut our hair. It took them about one minute to finish each head. The first barber gave three or four straight cuts with his old and squeaky clippers, from the neck up to the forehead. He then pushed his man into the hands of the other barber on the opposite side. The other fellow, sitting on a low stool, then shaved hair off the body with a rusty but very sharp razor. Hair piled up all over the place faster than it could be swept away, but still the S.S. barked their commands: "Quicker! Faster! Quicker!"

Out of the hands of the barbers we were herded into yet another room. Again came the same terrorizing procedure of pushing large numbers of men through a tiny connecting door. This time we were a little more careful and managed to reach the next room without giving the overanxious S.S. men much opportunity to lash out. The door behind us was tightly shut as we found ourselves in a gray-tiled hall, the ceiling of which was covered with showers.

"See those showers up there," said an elderly fellow, who had been lucky enough to escape Dr. Mengele's attention. "It's a fake. I heard about it. Not water, but GAS will come out of them."

My heart played queer tricks.

"Must be true," echoed another voice. "Look, there isn't a single S.S. man here. They are watching from the little window in the door."

And indeed they were keeping an eye on us from outside. But boiling water, not gas, began to stream out from the showers above us. We tried to escape the scalding water, but the spray was all over us. The S.S. man watching from the little window then turned ice-cold water on us, and without warning, he switched back to hot. I grabbed my shoes and put them over my head, thus partially alleviating my plight. Meanwhile I kept a close eye on Benzi Gottlieb and Baruch Stern, fearful of losing sight of them.

This "treatment" went on for about fifteen minutes, after which we were driven out, with the usual shouts, kicks, and knocks, into a fourth room. Here, at the exit door, stood two *Haeftlinge*, each with two buckets full of strong ammonia water at his feet. We had to pass them in a slow single file, in spite of the urgings and lashings of the S.S. men behind us, and we had to stop at the door. The *Haeftlinge* dipped a thick ladle into the bucket and splashed the liquid under our arms and between our legs. These parts, already red and sore from the razor-blades and hot shower, burned like hell as soon as the ammonia touched them.

Out in the next room, a longish hall, we had to run naked past a line of tables from which the *Haeftlinge* threw new clothes at us. First a vest, then a shirt, a pair of pants, so-called socks, trousers, a jacket, and a cap were hurled at us as we ran past each table. To drop one piece of clothing meant leaving it behind and being deprived of it. The S.S. particularly enjoyed this run. They wanted victims to drop the clothing, as indeed many did. But there was no way back.

"*Anziehn . . . Fertig machen!*" yelled the S.S. as we filed past the last table. They allowed us sixty seconds to get dressed on the spot. There was no time to look at the size of your trousers or for the buttons of your shirt. "Get on with it!" they yelled and, after the expiration of the time limit, we had to stand five deep in front of the exit. Baruch dropped his spectacles in the ensuing panic, and they broke as they fell on the stone floor. We had to hold him by the hand to make sure that he did not get himself into any trouble.

Then the door was thrown open and, to my horror, I discovered that night had fallen over the Death Cage of Auschwitz.

9

LIKE WELL-TRAINED animals we had got to the stage when we could anticipate our master's whistle. In silence we lined up five deep the moment we left the so-called House of Transformation. And indeed transformed we were as we stood in the cold, dark night. Rain was beginning to fall. We were demoralized, shaken, afraid, humiliated, and completely dehumanized. Again we were flanked by S.S. men who counted and recounted us like cattle, and finally marched us off in military fashion.

"*Links . . . Links!*" commanded the S.S. man leading our column. "Left, right! Left, right!" They marched us as though we were new recruits proceeding towards our barracks after having changed from mufti into new army uniforms.

I never knew I could feel so cold. My teeth rattled and my arms were shaking beyond control. My feet were numb. I felt that I had no blood left to circulate. It was not until I bent down that I noticed my "new" trousers were so short that they barely covered my knees. I had not had time to put on my socks; I had pushed them into my jacket pocket, and slipped my feet into my wet shoes.

As we marched along the dark and frightening passages between grim watchtowers and barbed-wire fences, I turned to Benzi who marched alongside of me.

"Benzi! I shall freeze to death."

"Don't panic," he said wisely. "My trousers are short too. But there will be plenty of men in our group whose trousers are too long for them. Once we reach our destination we'll sort everything out. In the meantime march briskly and swing your hands to and fro. That will keep your blood flowing."

This was sound advice. And as the weeks dragged by, Benzi proved himself to be a remarkable leader, a specialist in keeping up the morale of his friends, even during the tensest and most terrifying moments. It was a great comfort to have him near me. On this first night we passed gate after gate, turning left, right, and left again until finally at one gate the S.S. guards handed us over to a *Lager-Kapo,* himself an inmate, and left us.

The camp at which we arrived was the F-Lager, generally referred to as the "Zigeunerlager—Gipsies' Camp." Here, we were marched past long rows of black huts lining the roadway on both sides until we arrived at Block 14 which was empty. The huge interior was divided in the center by that inevitable long ledge. Worn out, we collapsed onto the cold stone floor. A few *Haeftlinge* came in now and again, looked us over suspiciously, and went out again. Then, in came the *Stubendienst* (room orderly). "Stand up!" he barked. "And remain standing!" We stood up.

Then at the shout of *"Achtung!"* the door burst open and in marched a well-dressed inmate with a well-padded overcoat and fur collar. He swung his walking stick about playfully as he paced up and down on top of the long brick ledge. Wordlessly he poked his stick viciously at anyone not standing at attention, or not having pulled off his cap from his clean-shaven head. Finally, turning in all directions like an auction-eer about to start the bidding, he asked: "Do you want anything?"

"Yes!" we chorused. "Could we have a drink of something?"

It was nearly thirty-six hours since we had had our last drink of water, and fear had parched our tongues.

"Ha, ha, ha!" he laughed, shaking his fat body forwards and backwards. "I think I forgot to tell you where you are!"

We were flabbergasted. Who was this little sadist with the Hungarian accent?

"I am your *Blockaeltester*," he said, as if guessing our thoughts. "You have arrived in the world's largest extermination camp. You are in Auschwitz! . . . Some of you came here with parents, or wives, or children, or brothers and sisters. Well, you must have seen the little square red-brick houses as you came in. You must have seen their short chimneys with the tongues of flame shooting out. Well, that is where they all are now—those who came here with you."

Stunned with shock by this hideous outburst, we stood like stone. This sub-human monster was obviously enjoying our reactions.

"So you want a drink, eh? Don't you know that human life is the most worthless commodity in this camp? Any S.S. man can shoot you down without reason; any *Kapo* can kill you without having to account for it. I, too, can beat you to death without let or hindrance. Now listen. I will kill anyone here who has smuggled anything into this camp! Hand everything over to me right here and now. You will be searched later. Anyone found hiding anything, anything at all, will be shot."

He waited patiently for a few minutes, viewing the lines carefully in case someone wanted to hand something over. Seeing that there was no response, he continued with a recital of the laws of the camp—the laws of the jungle.

"You stand to attention whenever you are addressed by an S.S. or *Lagerleader*. You remove your caps six steps before meeting an S.S. man, three steps before a *Kapo* or *Lageraeltester*." He gave us the various ranks and colors of the armbands of the privileged inmates: *Lageraeltester; Blockaeltester; Kapo; Stubendienst; Blockschreiber*, etc., etc., concluding with:

"There will be no food or drinks for you until tomorrow afternoon. At five A.M. you will stand to *Appell* outside the barrack. Any questions?"

"Any questions?" he roared madly.

"No!" came a solitary answer.

"Right," he said. "Lights out soon. Get to sleep."

"Where?" someone asked.

"On the floor," he yelled.

I breathed freely again when this *Blockaeltester* had gone, this brute who had attained his position at the expense of his fellow victims.

"Benzi," I pleaded desperately, as I sank to the floor, blue with cold, "for heaven's sake help me . . . I cannot bear it."

He pulled the so-called socks out of my pocket. They were two pieces of woolen material, cut away from our prayer shawl, the *Tallit*, and roughly sewn together. He rubbed my feet for a few minutes, put the socks on and then the shoes. Then he watched me closely, for I was still shivering.

"Here," he said, "come and stand yourself between Schiff and me."

Schiff was a jolly red-headed Viennese in his fortieth year. He was to share the rest of his camp-life in close company with Benzi and me. After a brief and very formal introduction, I warmed up between the hefty bodies of Benzi and Schiff.

Then the few lights in the barrack snapped out. Removing our shoes, we lay down on the cold and bare concrete floor with nothing to cover us. I remained tightly squeezed between my two friends.

"Warmer now?" Schiff inquired with a smile.

"A little," I said gratefully.

"Well," he joked, "the Viennese say 'lay down on your stomach, and cover yourself with your bottom.' "

In spite of the exhaustions and tribulations of the past days, sleep would not come. Too much had happened to us in these past few hours. The thought of what might be the fate of our dear ones would not leave us. Were they being pushed into those ghastly death chambers at this very second? "Oh God! Merciful God, please let them not suffer. . . . Make it quick and easy for them."

This constant dread, together with my anxiety for the future, brought on a fit of nervous ague. What will become of me? Will I be able to stand all that is ahead of me? Will it be possible to survive? What will they do to us when the Russians reach the camp? Would it not have been wiser if I had volunteered for "light work," and joined my parents? Quick death was a luxury in Auschwitz. My mind was in a seething turmoil; panic took hold of me again. I wanted to jump up and run, run run. . . .

"Grab hold of your shoes; they're trying to pinch them!" shouted someone in the pitch-dark barrack room.

Quickly I bent forward to reach for my shoes. They were still there. But others in the block began to cry out as they found their shoes had disappeared. The thieves, aided and abetted by the *Blockaeltester* and his *Stubendienst*, had taken their loot and disappeared under the cover of darkness. Shoes were very valuable in the camp, and the thieves knew that newcomers would be well shod. They must have had a good look around while the lights were on, and then pounced on the shoes when darkness fell. Some of the prisoners crawled about in the darkness, groping their way from man to man in search of the stolen shoes. There were shrieks and shouts as loose shoes were grabbed by owners and searchers alike. In the midst of this melee the *Blockaeltester* and his *Stubendienst*— judge and jury in their blocks—burst in, their torches flashing on the heaps of excited men.

"Shut your traps!" came a mad yell from the *Blockaeltester* as he lashed out indiscriminately. "There must be absolute silence in my block, or you will join your relatives."

Everyone returned hastily and quietly to his place. No one dared move. No one said another word as our first day in Auschwitz came to a close.

❖   ❖   ❖   ❖   ❖   ❖   ❖

A thunderous noise from the banging of a huge triangular gong hanging outside the block entrance brought us to our feet within seconds. The *Blockaeltester* occupied a small room at the entrance to the block. He was well supplied with the greatest luxuries in camp—food, liquor, and cigarettes—to say nothing of a fine divan.

He stormed into the barrack room. "Outside all of you, for *Appell!*"

We had no chance to wash, nor even use the toilet, which, in any case, was simply a dirty overfilled bucket. As I staggered into the fresh air—that is if you could ever call the foul-smelling air of Auschwitz fresh—it seemed as if the whole world around us was calling one word, and one word only: "*APPELL!*"

Every *Kapo*, every *Blockaeltester* and every *Stubendienst* in all the thousands of little blocks was shouting *Appell* over the noise of the heavy gongs.

"*Aufgehn zu Fuenf!*" The block-orderlies busied themselves. "Line up five deep."

I tried to identify some of the people lined up outside the block opposite us, but it was impossible. Indeed, I could hardly recognize Benzi or Baruch as I looked at them in the revealing light of day. We all looked bedraggled with our shaven heads and our dirty clothing. Benzi discovered he had been given a nightshirt instead of a shirt. The top button was missing. "At least it is long and warm," Benzi joked as he made the discovery.

The *Stubendienst* adjusted our lines in strict order. Short ones in front, taller ones behind, so that everyone could be seen by the inspecting S.S. man. Then the first man on the left in the front row had to shout "One" into the ears of the prisoner on the left, the second prisoner, turning his head smartly to the left to shout "Two," and so on to the end of the line. The *Stubendienst* took his time in multiplying the total by five, which gave him the number of inmates in his block. After some delay, the *Blockaeltester* came marching forward, his heavy black boots shining brightly, and counted us again, marching slowly along the line.

Then came the long, long wait for the S.S. man. We stood at ease, but were not allowed to talk. Some sank into the soft, muddy ground. The *Blockaeltester* threw Dutch wooden shoes at the shoeless ones after bullying them for not looking after their belongings.

"*Achtung! Muetzen Ab!*" he commanded as the inspecting *Unterschaarfuehrer* drew near. We stood rigidly at attention and pulled off our caps simultaneously.

The S.S. officer walked very deliberately along the lines, pointing with his gloved finger at every group of five, and directing his piercing eyes at every man in the column. He finished his count, wrote down the number on a piece of paper and walked smartly towards the next block.

"Now," we thought, "we can return to our block." But no! *Appell* lasted until the entire population of Auschwitz, estimated at that time to have been about two hundred thousand, had been counted and found correct. If one prisoner was missing, the whole procedure was repeated. Auschwitz, we learned, had known *Appells* lasting a whole day. Our first experience of it took about three to four hours, but none of us had a watch to tell the time exactly.

We never returned to Block 14. After a long period of waiting we were taken to Block 19 further up the foul camp road.

Auschwitz was a dread sight on that cold and misty morning. Miles upon miles of electrified barbed wire, about twenty feet high, encircled the entire camp, and separated one section from another. It was almost as difficult to get from Lager F into Lager D as it would have been to escape the camp itself. Three feet in front of the high barbed-wire fences was a short, knee-high fence. Guards in the watchtowers would shoot anyone trespassing beyond these two fences. The electrified wires were not always at full power; sometimes they were only at half-strength, causing grievous burns to anyone touching them. In one short walk I met prisoners from Russia, with the red triangle on their jackets, and prisoners from Rumania, Holland, Belgium, Czechoslovakia, Yugoslavia, Hungary, France, Italy, Poland, Bulgaria, Austria, Germany, and every other European country. But the overwhelming majority of all these nationals were Jews, with the yellow triangle as their mark.

To our surprise, Block 19 was flanked on both sides by rows of long wooden, three-tier bunks with some blankets on them. There was, of course, the inevitable long brick ledge straddling the center.

No sooner had the new *Blockaeltester* left us in the block than a number of inmates jumped from their bunks and began embracing and kissing. They were our friends from Bratislava who had come to Auschwitz with the previous transports. What a pathetic reunion it was! There was the familiar face of Jozsi Grunwald, a tiny little fellow; there was jolly Modche Fischhof; his brother-in-law, Gestetner; tubby little Hugo

Gross who looked naked without his pipe; fourteen-year-old Walti Braun who luckily had escaped Mengele's otherwise careful eyes; young Schmuli Rosenberg who also had escaped Mengele's selecting thumb—but, alas, not for long; Doctor Tauber, a short redhead; Akiba Simcha Ungar, a handsome young man and a promising rabbi. Then there were the intellectuals: Dr. Pal and his brother; fat Dr. Konig, the dentist; Dr. Glaser, the gynecologist, and his brother; Dr. J. Fischer, the rich spirit distiller, and his son.

Grunwald invited Benzi, Baruch, and me to his bunk, which although intended to accommodate four people, had to take eight. We settled down to talk about our experiences. I was still chilled, for I had not found anyone who was prepared to exchange trousers with me. Even those who did have trousers too long for their short legs preferred to hold on to them and enjoy that extra bit of warmth which the double turn-ups afforded them. I did not blame them.

Suddenly, from the entrance to the Block I heard my Hebrew name being called. There must have been plenty among the hundreds in that barrack whose name was the same as my own, but the voice was terribly familiar to me. I jumped down from my bunk and rushed towards the door.

"Simche . . . Simche!" the voice kept calling.

"Here I am," I answered. I pushed my way past the milling crowd in the block, until I came face-to-face with the owner of the well-known voice. We fell into each other's arms.

"Oh, my God," I exclaimed, still in embrace. "You look terrible. Where are your glasses?"

My brother-in-law, Romi, tried to smile. "You don't look too handsome yourself, Simche."

"How did you know I was here?" was my first question.

"I heard that a lot of Bratislavians were brought in yesterday; someone recognized you among them."

Suddenly we stood silent.

His voice was a whisper as he asked: "Where are the parents? Were they with you?"

I nodded my head. Then tears fell from both of us. He was the eldest son-in-law of the family, loved and highly respected for his intelligence and knowledge. He was like a son to my parents, and a brother to me.

"My goodness," he suddenly exclaimed, obviously trying to change the tragic subject. "Are these the trousers they gave you?"

He did not wait for an answer, but hastily removed a woolen scarf from his neck, tore it into two long pieces, and wrapped each one round my uncovered legs. Then he pulled a dirty little piece of black bread from his pocket, about the size of a Brazil nut, and gave it to me.

"But it's moldy," I protested.

"It's food!" he cut in. "A week from today you will be glad to find such a little piece. Just put it in your pocket. Bread never gets uneatable in this camp. . . ."

Shouts were now echoing all over the camp. *"Kaffee holen! Brot holen!"* From every block three or four specially privileged inmates joined up to fetch the coffee and the bread.

"Try to get among the bread fetchers," Romi advised me. "There is always a chance of 'organizing' an extra portion for yourself."

"Organisieren," was the camp's special word for stealing, bartering, exchanging, or finding anything extra. But I was not hungry for food just then. All I wanted to know was the fate of my sister, Ilonka, and her five children, the eldest of whom was only eight.

In a choking voice, his eyes streaming with tears, Romi told me the story of their capture and transportation to Auschwitz, via Sered. "I should have gone with them," he lamented. "I should not have left Ilonka alone to face this terrible fate with the children . . . I cannot forgive myself."

[97]

I tried to comfort him, but a sudden yell of "*Achtung!*" brought our conversation to an abrupt end. Romi rushed out of the door like lightning as Mengele swept into the block with an S.S. escort.

10

A LONG and heavy silence fell upon the entire block as the most hated man in Auschwitz concentrated his gaze upon us, while a couple of *Kapos* busied themselves among the crowd of terror-stricken inmates, ordering us to form a single line around the brick ledge.

"What does this mean?" I whispered to Jozsi Grunwald, who stood in front of me.

"Psht!" he murmured from the side of his mouth. "It's another *selection*. Don't talk, you may draw attention to yourself . . . and me."

"Can't we hide in the bunks?" I persisted quietly, ignoring his warning.

"*Kapo* will beat you to death if he finds you . . . I told you to shut up!"

Seconds later Mengele motioned with his head, and the *Kapos* shepherded us past him in a slow single line. As we approached him we had to strip to the waist and lower our trousers to the knees. Now and again Mengele would pull a prisoner from the line and order him into a corner behind a line of S.S. men. He stopped a youngster in the group.

"How old are you?"

"Seventeen," answered the boy shakily.

"How old are you?" Mengele repeated, somewhat louder.

"Seventeen."

"How old? . . ."

The boy's nerve broke. "Fourteen, but I can work . . . I am strong. I can work!" screamed the child as he sensed the shadow of death creeping nearer.

Mengele let him go, but pulled out the man behind him, although he looked perfectly fit. When Benzi stood before him and let down his trousers, Mengele barked: "Have you had a hernia?" "No," answered Benzi. There was a soul-chilling pause and then Mengele dismissed him.

Baruch, Grunwald, and I followed. My eyes were fastened on Mengele's thumb—the thumb that had signalled countless thousands to the gas chambers; the thumb that swung like a pendulum between life and death; the thumb that had sent my parents and my sister and her children to their doom. Mengele looked down at me, his thumb hesitating. Just when I thought my end had come, Fischhof, who was standing impatiently behind me, overanxious to get through the ordeal, gave me an involuntary push. I stumbled forward—and was through. I could hardly breathe, the suspense had been so dreadful.

When we had all passed him, Mengele turned round to count the "selected." He counted them, counted again, and then swung round like lightning. "One has escaped," he yelled at the S.S. men, who were supposed to have guarded the group.

"Line them up again!" he screamed at the *Kapos*. "I'll recognize the fugitive in a flash. Nobody escapes my eyes. Nobody!"

Mengele was now in a raging temper, and the faces in the crowd paled. Although the *Kapos* used their sticks and boots like flails in an effort to get us into line again, they weren't fast enough for the fuming destroyer.

"I'll find him," Mengele howled afresh. "It's the dark thin one with the glasses. . . . Get them on the move!"

My heart pounded as I heard these words. I fitted that description accurately. With trembling fingers I removed my spectacles and drew a deep breath to fill up my stomach, then I prayed silently as the lines moved along, much faster than during the first call-up. But I never reached Mengele. He pulled out a youngster from the line whom I recognized immediately as Shmuli Rosenberg, a schoolmate of mine. He was certainly not the one who escaped, if there was an escape at all. Shmuli, a redhead, had never worn glasses, but apparently Mengele had detected a bullet wound on Shmuli's chest and that was excuse enough to whisk him away.

Poor Shmuli! I remembered, as they marched him out with the others towards the main gates, how he had received his wound. In the autumn of 1940 when he was only fourteen, a group of Hitlerites broke into his house in the middle of the night, poured petrol on his bed, and fired a gun at the escaping figure. Police and firemen arrived. Shmuli was taken to the hospital and an arrest was made. The culprit, a former caretaker whom Shmuli's father had dismissed from his job many years earlier because of theft, wanted to take revenge on his former boss. He mistook the bedrooms and thought that he had set fire to the old man's bed and killed him. The doctors saved Shmuli's life, but could not remove the bullet; it had gone too deep. Once or twice every year Shmuli had to be rushed to the hospital as the wandering bullet threatened to touch his heart. So now Shmuli, whose life had once been saved miraculously, was to forfeit it in the gas chamber.

As soon as the S.S. left us, I rushed to the toilet which was situated at the far end of the barrack, behind the blocks. A man sat outside it. He was called the *Scheissmeister*, and they said in Auschwitz that the *Scheissmeisters* had the safest jobs and lived the longest. The toilet, which was also a block, was flanked on both sides with latrines and had a narrow pipe running in the center throughout its length. From it spouted thin jets of water which the *Scheissmeister* warned us were poisonous and not to be used for drinking. After I had relieved myself for the first time in three days, I realized that there was no toilet paper. I called to the *Scheissmeister*. Shrugging his shoulders, he gave me to understand that there was no paper in the whole of Auschwitz, and that I would have to "find another way out." I tore off a piece from my scarf and washed it after use. I retained this little piece throughout my days in Auschwitz; others did likewise. This surely was the most calculated humiliation that the Nazi monsters could devise: you were not only treated like animals but you were expected to behave like them.

When I returned to the block, six huge barrels of the size and appearance of old and dirty dustbins were brought in. They contained a thick gray mixture, misnamed soup. One dirty and rusty tin bowl was given to every four inmates to share their soup. There were no spoons. All four had to hold on to the bowl as the line moved toward the *Blockaeltester* who supervised the serving. The stinking mixture was then sloshed into the bowl, and the next group motioned forward. Benzi, Baruch, Schiff, and I stood transfixed as we watched some of the starving prisoners heave and pull the bowl to and fro in order to get their share. Some poked their hands in it and licked their fingers. We did not eat. The smell and the sight of it made me sick and even Benzi, who did try to eat some, turned his face away and retched. Some inmates from other blocks—those who knew that newcomers never ate their food for a day or two—came in, hoping that they could grab an extra portion of the swill, "*Nachschlag*," as they called it. We soon parted with our bowl, and I watched with amazement as Dr. Tauber finished his portion to the last drop. He noticed my amazement and came over to me.

"Listen my boy," he said, as he wiped his lips with his bare hands. "You are not at home, and nobody will care a hoot whether you eat your food or not. But as a friend and admirer of your father, and as a doctor, I think I ought to warn you that unless you eat every scrap of food given to you, you will have no chance at all of survival. And that goes for you fellows, too." He turned to Benzi, Baruch, and Schiff. "If you ever want to leave this bloody place alive you must eat what they give you—and try to organize more, if you can."

As the evening drew near, a few of us gathered between the bunks for the Friday evening service. Yes, it was Sabbath again, and as I began to whisper the familiar words of the Sabbath Eve Service, I was lulled by a feeling of tranquillity. Gone were the panic and tension that had overwhelmed me these past few days. I discovered for the first time in my life the real power and value of prayer and faith in God. I could feel my words shattering the iron gates and the high-powered fences, going past the hundreds of guards, dugouts, and watchtowers, out into the open, and reaching towards heaven. Here, I knew, was a way of escape, a source of strength and a means of survival of which no power on earth could deprive me.

I felt confident and serene as I squeezed my thin body into the overcrowded bunk between Benzi and Schiff, with Grunwald, Baruch Stern, Gestetner, Fischhof, and young Walti Braun sharing it. We spread the three thin blankets evenly over us and settled down for the night. Each of us slept on his left side, thus making more room and preventing his having to breathe into his bunkmate's face. If one turned, all had to turn; if one moved, all had to move. Crammed together like sardines we found comfort and companionship in our common misery, and soon the blessing of sleep blotted out the horrors of our plight.

I ate everything that was given to me the next day. Not only did I swallow the thick, horrible soup—although I had to force it down me like a foul medicine—but I also ate my portion of bread, a fifth of a short and heavy black loaf, and drank what was called coffee. In none of the other camps that I had the misfortune to pass through was this evil brew so sickening as in Auschwitz. The liter of dark grey fluid that smelled and tasted like boiled-over dishwater could have contained anything but coffee. The strong lacing of bromide could be detected both in the soup and in the coffee. But I drank it, again sharing a rusty tin bowl with Benzi, Baruch Stern, and Schiff.

We needed the coffee, after yet another three-hour Appell, on the rainy and windy Sabbath morning, which had not gone off as smoothly as the previous one. As we stood outside, anticipating the arrival of the *Unterschaarfuehrer* at any moment, there came a sudden deep and frightening groan from the line behind me. Turning round, I saw Federweiss, the man who had tried to chisel his way out of the fast-moving cattle truck on the way to Auschwitz, sink slowly to the ground, his face deathly pallid, and his mouth foaming with saliva.

"He is an epileptic," called Dr. Tauber, who stood nearby. "Try to force his fists open, it might revive him." But there was no time to work on Federweiss's tightly clenched hands.

"*Achtung!*" yelled the Blockaeltester. "*Muetzen Ab!*"

Standing in the front line I turned my face forward and stood at rigid attention as the S.S. man paced along the line to take the count.

As he reached me I gasped with relief, for he had passed Federweiss's line without noticing anything. Turning my face slightly over to the right, I saw the unconscious body of Federweiss propped up straight, squeezed tightly between the bodies of the two men in front and behind him. The man in the rear held him up by his trousers, while the one in front pushed his back on Federweiss's chest to prevent him from dropping. They kept these positions for quite a while—indeed until the S.S. man and the *Blockaeltester* with his *Stubendienst* were at a safe distance. Afterwards, we got to work on him, and revived him soon enough. He did not know what had happened, and said that he never had an epileptic attack in his life.

Romi came over to me on the following day, a clear but cold Sunday afternoon.

"Come with me quickly," he urged, as he pulled me by the arm, leading me down the road into another block. He took me between two bunks, and pulled out a pair of *Tefillin* from under the blankets, bidding me put them on.

"Just say the *Shema*, and take them off again," he whispered as I tied the black leather straps around my left arm. I made the blessings, said the first section of the *Shema*, took the *Tefillin* off again and within seconds was out on the road again.

I felt uplifted as I set out with Romi for a little stroll: glad to be with my brother-in-law again, and grateful for the opportunity of putting *Tefillin* on my arm and head in the charnel house of Auschwitz. This ceremony had meant a lot to me, and I admired the courage of the stranger who had smuggled these *Tefillin* into the camp. He had risked his life for them. The Nazis could kill men, but they could not kill courage. Had the stranger smuggled in a hundred cigarettes in place of the *Tefillin*, he could have lived the life of a prince. Who can do justice in words to this wonderful act of faith?

As we walked along, Romi and I speculated about what would happen to us: Would we be sent from Auschwitz? Everyone in the camp had to go to work. Now that we had by-passed the gas chambers, should we be put to work here or in some German labor camp? There were daily calls for inmates to join the *Arbeits-Kolonnen* in the nearby coal mine in Gleiwitz, or similar places. I knew, however, that I could never survive the inhuman conditions of the coal mines, and in any case I wanted to get as far away as possible from Auschwitz and its gas chambers. Romi, too, was hoping he would be transferred to a German labor camp.

Suddenly a wild cry made us turn round. A man from my block, a dentist, had flung himself with outstretched arms against the high-tension barbed wires. With an agonizing cry he fell back on the ground, his burned arms clawing the air, his body writhing in agony. The power in the fences was not at full strength, so the poor man's attempt to end his life resulted only in severe burns to his hands. I wanted to rush over to him and pull him towards the barracks, but Romi held me back.

"Look at that guard up in the watchtower," he warned me. "He will fire at anyone crossing over the short protective fence."

I glanced up at the trigger-happy killer high up in his hut. He had turned his machine gun in our direction and was awaiting developments. Nobody dared move, but I could no longer bear the cries of the injured man. I bade Romi a quick good-bye, and rushed back to my block.

Dr. Horvath, a City Councillor in pre-war Bratislava, met me at the entrance. He, too, had witnessed the scene outside. He looked desperate and shaken.

"How can God allow all this?" he demanded of me angrily. "I have known your parents for many years. Your father was one of the most righteous men I ever knew. He was a rabbi, a man who devoted his life to the service of God. Is it right that his life should have ended so cruelly over there?" He pointed towards the ever-smoking chimneys of the crematoria.

"I do not know the answer to these questions," I said quietly, "but I feel sure my father would not have asked them, if he were here with us. Questions will not help us," I continued. "They will only destroy our morale. You must keep your trust in God! You will never regret it."

I tried hard to inject some hope into this dejected man, but it was of no avail. I had pity for Dr. Horvath. I realized that he had neither the physical strength nor the spiritual convictions to survive a hell like Auschwitz. Without these qualities there was little hope of survival.

These experiences awoke in me a sense of appreciation and deep gratitude to my parents for the upbringing they had given me. I was lucky to have had a father who guided me in the way of God, and who instilled in me so much religious conviction. I was now reaping the benefit of that upbringing and could face these grave and challenging days with hope based on trust in God. I recalled how Father used to say in his quiet and gentle way: "Don't worry, there is a great God above us. He will surely help." He said these words so often, and with so much conviction, that they still rang in my ears. I wanted to hold on to these words and carry them with me wherever fate would take me.

But, ever in my mind—it had now become an obsession—was the problem of getting away from Auschwitz as quickly as possible. My heart quaked when, the following morning, my brother-in-law, Romi, came bursting into my block, his face as white as a ghost.

MY BROTHER-IN-LAW's eyes were cold and devoid of expression. I fought down the shock his appearance had given me. Something ghastly must have happened, for I knew Romi was not one to panic easily.

"I can't stay . . . I came to say good-bye," he burst out. "I . . . I've run away."

I grabbed both his hands in an effort to steady his nerves. "Run away!" I echoed. The words sounded so impossible, so fantastic, in a cage like Auschwitz that I feared Romi's reason had given way. "What . . . what do you mean?"

"They picked two hundred from my block for *Sonder Kommando*," he jerked out. "I was among them. I made a bolt for it as the column reached the gates. There's only one thing left. I must get on the Braunschweig transport before they catch me. It leaves today."

"But what is the *Sonder Kommando?*" I asked in bewilderment.

My question remained unanswered for Romi tore himself

from my grip, and with a quick embrace and a kiss, was out of the block. Gone! Gone forever.

Other prisoners in the block, however, soon put me wise. *Sonder Kommandoes,* they explained tersely, were those who had been picked to work in the gas chambers and the crematoria. Theirs was the worst job in the world, in any age. They had to drag out the bodies from the gas chambers, remove their gold teeth, if any, tear out their hair and wrench off any artificial limbs, and then cart the remains to the crematoria. Nobody really knew all of their duties, but they knew the *Sonder Kommandoes* were treated well and received extra rations while working; they also knew that after three or four weeks, they too would be pushed without warning into the gas chambers for final liquidation while a new group was hastily picked. Those few who, by a miracle of miracles, did manage to escape from the grisly gang, never dared admit in camp that they were *Sonder Kommandoes.* Nevertheless, sufficient evidence of the horror and terror surrounding their jobs sneaked through to scare every inmate away from being chosen for the ghastly *Sonder Kommando.*

Those beastly S.S. refused to touch the victims of their own murders. Inspired by barbaric cruelty unprecedented in history, yet filled with cowardice, they ordered inmates to complete the final liquidation and remove the corpses of the innocent victims slaughtered daily by the thousands entirely without reason or motive. In their thirst for cruelty and horror, the S.S. monsters enjoyed watching the men of the *Sonder Kommando* going insane at the sight of their own wives or children in the mass of tightly-clinched gassed bodies.

Never have I met greater cowards than these trained S.S. men, once their rifles or guns were taken from them. You rarely saw a victim in the death cage of Auschwitz falling on his knees before an S.S. man to plead for his life, or the lives of his family. But I saw, on the day of liberation, hundreds of these very same S.S. men pleading, crying, and begging on their knees in a vain attempt to save their heartless lives. They whined for *mercy:* the word which they themselves rubbed out of their dictionaries and refused to grant even to innocent babies.

No wonder then that Romi had chosen to escape the column of freshly selected *Sonder Kommandoes,* even at the risk of getting a round of machine-gun fire into his body from one of the guards in the watchtowers.

Romi's luck held out for a while. He did manage to get on the Braunschweig transport. There, I was told after the war, he shared his jokes, his food, and his unshakable trust in God with many of his fellow inmates until the morning of January 24, 1945, when he collapsed at *Appell* never to rise again.

To me, his escape was a disastrous blow. All my hopes of joining up with Romi, my only close relative in the camp, had crashed in one unexpected moment. I rejoined my friends in the bunk, shaking like a leaf. I whispered to Benzi that we had better try and find out about the prospects of getting into a transport. Otherwise, we too would be selected for the dread *Sonder Kommando.*

Benzi set about the problem immediately.

One of the handful of Bratislavian girls who had come to Auschwitz in 1942 and were still alive was Regina Hofstadter. She was a *Block-Schreiber,* and was thus able to move about more freely from camp to camp. She was always ready to be helpful, and Benzi went in search of her. She was not able to give him the details of any particular transport which she could recommend, but she warned him that it was always preferable to join a transport where civilians did the selecting rather than those which were selected by S.S. men. One thing she was quite sure about: "Try and get as far away from Auschwitz as you possibly can."

No sooner was Benzi back from his exploration tour than we

were all taken out of the block and marched away without any explanation. Fears of the *Sonder Kommando* immediately rose in our minds as we left the F-Lager. At the C-Lager, however, we were herded into one of the blocks.

"Have you ever heard of Pinkus?" asked the *Blockaeltester*, a fat, thick-set little man with a huge shovel in his hand, as he mounted the long chimney inside the block to greet his new lodgers.

"I am Pinkus!" he proclaimed proudly, and raising both his hands and his shovel skyward, declared: "These hands have sent many people up to heaven. But if you behave yourselves you have nothing to fear."

No sooner had he finished his boastful introduction than he began to hit out madly with the shovel at anyone who dared to enter his block with muddy shoes.

"Mine is the cleanest block in Auschwitz," he screamed. "I mean to keep it that way! Anyone entering the block with dirty shoes dies!"

Pinkus was obviously a madman. He kept us out of the block for the best part of the day, and upon entering, we had to take off our shoes. As in most other blocks, there were huge posters on the walls reading: *"Eine Laus Dein Tod!"* ("One louse means your death.") And indeed none of the *Blockaelteste* took the *Laeuse-Kontrolle* (lice-control) as seriously as Pinkus. I did not even know what a louse looked like, let alone where to find one. But Pinkus subjected us to three lice-controls and looked for them thoroughly. He searched particularly the corners of the shirt buttonholes and under the seams. To our relief he never found any.

C-Lager bordered the women's camp. Two high wire fences, with room left in the center for the watchful S.S. patrols and their Alsatians to pass through comfortably, divided the sexes. I was shocked as I looked across into the women's camp. Were it not for the fact that they wore dresses, it would have been difficult to distinguish them from the men. Their heads were as clean-shaven as ours. They wore striped prison uniforms or dresses—old shabby rags with huge squares cut out in the back and replaced by striped material.

I could see that the women were worse off than we were. The S.S. women were more vicious and brutal. In many cases they were envious and jealous of the good-looking Jewish girls, and took their spite out on them. I called over to the girls asking where they came from. They were glad to exchange a few shouts with the men across the road, even at the risk of getting a beating from their warders. But all the girls there were Hungarians, and I knew none of them.

As a young Talmud pupil I once heard my teacher say that whoever made *Kiddush Levanah* (the blessing of the new moon) was sure to survive that month without any fatal mishap to himself. Throughout the war years I remembered these words, and never missed making the blessing a few days after the beginning of the Jewish month.

On this particular evening in Auschwitz, looking out from Pinkus' block I saw the moon peeping out occasionally between fast-moving clouds. Come what may, I told myself, I must get out there for a couple of minutes to make the blessing.

It was cold, and the ground was muddy from the rain that had fallen all day, as I made my way quietly out of the block. I waited a few minutes until some of the dark clouds passed by, and then as soon as the shape of the moon became visible, I recited the prayers. I was carried away by devotion and deep feeling as I came to the passage in which we pray that just as we cannot reach the moon, so our foes and enemies should not be able to reach us. This passage was particularly apt and significant in these fateful days, and I repeated it often, as if trying to envelop myself in a spiritual armor which no one could penetrate. That night I repeated this sentence again and again until a shout of "Halt!" brought me to a frightened stop.

An S.S. man, garbed in a long fur coat, the collar of which reached right up to his ears, noticed me as he patrolled the narrow passage between the men's and women's camp. I remained still, but when I saw him lift the rifle off his shoulders I made a quick dash into the block. To my horror, however, I found that I had lost one shoe. The other must have stuck in the mud outside. There I was in Pinkus' sanctuary with one dirty shoe and one shoeless foot. I waited fearfully for a few minutes hoping that the S.S. man would move further away so that I could recover my missing shoe, and also that Pinkus would not come out of his comfortable little room at the entrance to the block. To be caught by either of the two would have meant certain death—by rifle or by shovel. After some long, palpitating minutes, I ventured out again and recovered my shoe.

But how pleased I was, very pleased and content, that I had been able to make the blessing. I felt as if I had just received a new lease on life, even if only for the duration of the month.

But three weeks in Auschwitz was a lifetime. The crematoria, all four of them, were burning day and night. Only God knew how many men, women, and children were consumed by the flames every twenty-four hours. To be safe for three long weeks was worth much more than the risk I stood.

The next few days we went "job hunting." Calls for *Arbeitseinsatz Antretten* (voluntary labor parties) were made every few hours. But we did not join anything. We got used to the *Appells,* to the daily rations which grew smaller and smaller every day, and waited for the sign of a good transport to come along. We even went out tobacco hunting. Five of us joined forces to search for tiny remnants of cigarettes dropped by S.S. men, *Kapos,* or *Blockaelteste.* In two days we had collected enough to make up one small cigarette, the size of half an ordinary cigarette. We rolled the strands of tobacco together and enjoyed a little smoke, taking turns to have a pull.

On Thursday morning, exactly one week after our arrival, we heard that there was a civilian in the camp looking for laborers for a factory in Germany.

"We cannot push our luck too far," said Benzi as the news reached the block. "I suggest we volunteer!"

Accordingly, about 150 from our block went out to line up in front of a tall German civilian accompanied by two S.S. men. The *Lager Kapo* called for *Arbeits-Einsatz* and men from various blocks came to join the huge line that was forming outside.

The civilian walked along our line which stood at attention five deep, and nodded his apparent approval to the S.S. men.

"I want four hundred and fifty," he said, and stepped backwards to let the S.S. do the selecting.

The "selection" stopped dead before me. Benzi, Baruch, Grunwald, Schiff, Fischhof, Dr. Tauber, and most of the others were in the group. The rest of us were ordered back into the barracks.

I was panic-stricken. Benzi, my best friend, and last remaining prop, had gone with the others. They all looked helplessly towards me while I stared back at them with a pounding heart and tear-filled eyes.

Never shall I know where I plucked the courage from, but ignoring the presence of the S.S., I ran after the slowly-moving column and squeezed myself into the line between Benzi and Schiff.

"Well done," whispered Benzi as he pressed my arm tightly.

I was quiet. The danger was not yet past. I knew that the real test would come when we reached the first gate and the guard would be ordered to count out 450 men. What would happen when they found 451 men? Of course they might not pick on me, but was it right that I should push someone else out on my own selfish account? Perhaps someone had noticed me; someone must have noticed me joining up and was wait-

[114]

ing to expose me. My mind raced faster than the column marched until we stopped dead.

The S.S. guard counted us twice. By some miracle it was 450 on the first count, and 450 on the second. The gates were opened and out we marched. I felt triumphant. Now it was my turn to press Benzi's hand in congratulations.

I shall never know what had happened. Maybe the S.S. man had made a mistake when he first counted us. Maybe someone in the group was as anxious to get out in the last moment as I was to get in. Or maybe this was just one of the many unexplainable miracles which every Auschwitz inmate came across during his stay there. Whatever the reason was, I was wild with joy to be back with my friends, and terribly relieved to be soon leaving Auschwitz, even though our group was then marched back into the dreaded F-Lager.

On the following morning we were taken into the "*Sauna*" (the baths), where, as on our arrival, our clothing was taken away and we were ordered into a bath. The gray hot water in the huge basin smelled strongly of disinfectants and we had to dip in, shoes and all, for a final clean-up. As we struggled out, we again underwent a thorough searching, in case we were trying to smuggle anything OUT of Auschwitz. Then each of us was given a new set of clothing. This time, the inmates were given a little more time, and they managed to size up every customer before supplying him with a shirt, a jacket, a pair of pants, a pair of trousers, a cap, and—what was most important —a coat. I was given a long and very warm winter coat. I wrapped it around me with the same delight a woman must feel on putting on her first mink coat.

Word must have gone round that this transport to Germany was a good one, for inmates came to us from various parts of the camp asking whether anyone would like to "change places" with them. This was probably the way Romi had managed to get on the Braunschweig transport a few days earlier. Needless to say, none of us moved. All the eighty-odd Bratislavians in the transport remained in one group, and we had a feeling that somehow we would manage to stay together until the train left Auschwitz. Benzi, Baruch, Schiff, Grunwald, Gestetner, Dr. Tauber, Dr. Pal, Dr. Konig, Herlinger, Weinberger, Hugo Gross, young Walti Braun, Fischhof, Dr. Fischer and son, and the rest of us stood hopefully together in one group on that Friday afternoon, never forgetting that we might have volunteered for a camp worse than Auschwitz. Was it to be out of the frying pan and into the fire?

12

WHEN NIGHTFALL came, we huddled together apprehensively in a corner for the Sabbath Eve prayers. We knew from bitter experience that Friday evenings were specially selected for anti-Jewish outbreaks in every Nazi-occupied country with many prison camps.

I think the reason for choosing Friday evenings was that the Germans knew that the Jews feel happy and released on their Sabbath, and from that day draw their inspiration, strength, and courage for the rest of the week. Either in envy or pure spite, the Nazis were determined to destroy that feeling of religious well-being.

Throughout the war years every Friday evening was signalled: by beating-up of Jews in the street; by ransacking of synagogues; by breaking into the few remaining Jewish shops; and by smashing windows in the ghetto. These Friday evening nightmares were especially enjoyed by the Nazis after it was no longer possible to surprise the Jews with any more mass arrests and deportations to labor camps.

The more the Germans planned to spoil our Sabbath, the

more we were determined to cling to it. Even as we stood, tense and nervous, in the death cage of Auschwitz on this particular evening, anxiously awaiting our next orders, we had no intention of denying ourselves the consolation of prayer.

Though the Jew was counted the cheapest and most worthless being in Auschwitz, it seemed strange to me that as we were marched out of F-Lager towards our uncertain destination, we were considered so important and precious. We were counted, recounted, checked, and double-checked at the approach of every one of the endless gates leading from the camp proper towards the railway line, as though the loss of one of us would be a world-shaking calamity.

With great joy and hope, I observed the train—those inevitable cattle trucks—whitewashed on both sides with the slogan, "Danger! Political Prisoners,"—standing at a distance. How wonderful to see the engine pointed away from the camp, instead of facing it.

It was a clear, icy evening as we paraded along a line of tables laden with food where our rations were to be handed out. Every prisoner was given one whole heavy black loaf, one ounce of ersatz honey, six ounces of wurst, and one ounce of margarine.

Benzi said "Good!" as he tucked his loaf of bread under his winter coat.

"What's so good about it?" I demanded.

Benzi turned to me in surprise. "Don't you see that one whole loaf of bread means we are going on a long trip?" His face brightened. "And a long trip means far away from Auschwitz."

His delight spread to me. "Yes, a whole loaf of bread also means that we shall be able to make *Kiddush* this evening and tomorrow on a whole bread. That's also worth something."

"Sure," Benzi agreed. "Tonight we shall eat yours, and tomorrow we shall eat mine. Baruch's we may keep untouched until the third meal tomorrow."

[118]

The immediate future seemed bright, but it soon darkened when our names were taken down by an S.S. officer, and fifty of us were crammed into each wagon, along with two S.S. men.

It was pitch-dark inside the wagon, and we had to feel our way around. I held on tightly to Benzi, Baruch held on to me, Schiff on to Baruch, and so on, until we finally managed to maneuver ourselves into a sitting position. Then someone shouted that his margarine had been stolen. We quickly made a check on our own rations. I poked into my pockets. The margarine, honey and wurst were there, but the loaf from my other pocket was missing. I cried like a child whose favorite toy has been snatched away by a big bully.

"Never mind, you can share mine," said Benzi generously.

"No, I won't . . . I can't take your food. I shall go and look for it. It must be in this wagon."

The two S.S. guards had split us into two sections of twenty-five, while they themselves sat on a small bench near the huge sliding doors. The passage between the two doors on both sides of the wagon had to be left completely free for them. This meant we had to cramp together even more tightly and thus lose sitting room. No sooner had I straightened myself up ready to search for my missing loaf than one of the S.S. flashed his torch into my face.

"Stepping out for a beer?" he demanded sarcastically.

"I'm looking for my . . . " I stopped suddenly, realizing that if I were to report the stolen bread, the S.S. might "enjoy" making a search for it, and someone might pay for it with his life. I quickly sat down.

"You there!" the S.S. man yelled, his torch still on my face. "Where did you want to go? What were you looking for?"

"I was . . . I was looking for a more comfortable place. There is hardly any room here."

"Perhaps you would like a divan brought in here, or a sleeping berth with hot and cold water?"

My lips were tight but my legs were trembling.

"You will remain standing where you are now," he ordered. "The rest will remain sitting until daybreak."

It must have been two hours before the train moved out of the siding. My legs were like lead, and the fear of having to remain standing the long night through filled me with horror. I knew I might collapse.

Suddenly, the train pulled out with a violent jerk, which threw me onto a heap of prisoners, causing an upheaval in the otherwise silent wagon. The S.S. jumped to their feet, and, with torchlights scanning the wagon, they ordered everyone to "keep down." That was lucky for me. I stayed down, too.

As the train gathered speed I thought of our previous train journey just ten days before; I thought of my parents, and all the other people who were with us but who were no longer alive. The cold draft from the small windows and from the gaps near the doors recalled what must have been my mother's last complaint. How unhappy she was when she found that she had left her warm woolen scarf in the old castle at Mariathal. Poor Mama, she needed no scarf now, woolen or otherwise. For the first time I really felt free to think back and wonder at what had happened to my family. Did Mama really deserve this dreadful end? She was the noblest and bravest woman on earth—the finest mother any child could have had. How she cared for us all; how she adored and esteemed Father. Her love and life was for him and her children—nothing else mattered. Furs, jewels, expensive clothes, were extravagances meant for, and wanted only, by other women. She never mentioned them.

Then I thought of Father. As a child I used to cry in bed at the thought that one day he would have to die. Now that he had gone I had hardly shed a tear. What had happened to me and all the rest of the men in the wagon? Were we all being transported in cattle-trucks because we really behaved like animals? Where was that human compassion of ours? Were all compassion, all love, and all nobility left in the "House of Transformation" in the death camp there, together with our made-to-measure suits, freshly laundered shirts, silk ties, and wrist watches?

I thought of the Friday evenings at home, with Father sitting majestically at the head of the Sabbath table and with the eyes of all of us turned warmly towards him. Were other fathers also like him? No. I was sure that he could have escaped the "Selection" ordeal had he not concerned himself with Mama's welfare. It seemed as if when he got to Auschwitz he was resolved to repay her for all her kindness, for her devotion, and for the sacrifices she had gladly made throughout her life.

Doctors told me after the war that death in the gas chambers was slow and very painful. The Germans—may they never be forgiven—used gas very sparingly in the latter part of 1944, which meant their defenceless victims had to struggle until they died. Many, the doctors told me, died in the arms of their children or wives. I'm sure Father must have made Mama's last moments easier and more acceptable. He must have spoken to her in his soft and gentle way of God, of His Will, and of the world to come. Oh yes, I could well picture them together in those final moments of their life. They never argued or quarrelled. They adored and esteemed one another throughout their married life. They belonged together, and left this world together. Father and his Mammele, as he affectionately called her, are sure to remain together until the end of all time.

Unconsciously I poked into my pocket for a handkerchief to wipe away my tears. This brought me back from my dreams. All I possessed in life was the margarine, the honey, and the wurst. No handkerchief. That luxury had gone with everything else. Meanwhile, the train gathered speed, taking us into yet another place of perhaps greater uncertainty.

Most of the prisoners appeared to be sleeping, tired out from the exertions of the day. Benzi, Schiff, Stern, and the rest had dozed off. I began to hum the beautiful songs which we used to sing at home at the Sabbath table, and eventually, accompanied by the clock-like hammering of the fast turning wheels, I too dozed off.

At the break of dawn the S.S. ordered us on our feet for *Appell.* It all seemed a bad joke to us. They shoved all fifty of us into one corner and then ordered us to file past in a single line towards the other corner. That was how they counted us. Taking no chances, they paraded us on *Appell* morning and evening and with German efficiency entered a full report into their handbooks after every count.

When *Appell* was over we were allowed to use the "rusty bucket." For the rest of the day it was out-of-bounds . . . that is, except for our masters, the S.S., who spent most of their time eating, drinking, and smoking and were in need of "the bucket" much more than their starved captives. Whenever the S.S. men had to make use of it, the rest of the men in the wagon had to turn around and face the wall in order not to embarrass the gentlemen of Hitler's Master Race.

Thirst was our greatest enemy in that stuffy wagon. While the S.S. men emptied one bottle of beer after another into their fat bellies, we were left hoping that the journey would soon come to an end, and that we would be able to quench our thirst for water and fill our lungs with fresh air.

We spent most of the day talking about the past or making new friends. We did not speak about the future. The immediate future now seemed very dark and hopeless, and a discussion of it would have served only to dishearten us further. Some of the prisoners kept their eyes firmly on the ever-chewing S.S. men in the hope of catching some discarded apple peelings or cigarette ends. I never went near them. I would have rather stayed without food than pick up any leftovers from the feet of those two killers. The S.S. enjoyed slinging their cigarette ends or salami skins on the floor and watching the inmates fight for them like ducks in a pond. Yet I did not blame them. They might have been hungrier and more in need of food than I.

By Sunday midnight the two S.S. guards were drunk and fed up with the lot of us. At first they started to bully us, and insisted on absolute silence. Even coughing or sneezing was forbidden. Then they got us to our feet and made us march in circles in the evil-smelling and pitch-dark wagon, with their torchlights wandering from man to man. Eventually they tired of this too, and changing their stiff attitude, asked whether there was one in the crowd who could tell a few jokes to make the time pass quicker.

Fischhof volunteered without hesitation. The crowd was hushed: not only the drunken S.S. but also the worn-out in-mates were anxious to get a little break, and Modche Fischhof was always a good comedian.

"Once an old man went to the doctor complaining that he had difficulty in passing water," Modche started, in his usual style.

"Let me have a specimen," said the doctor, handing the old man a bottle. The old man filled it in no time, and even let it overflow onto the carpet in the doctor's private surgery.

"Hey," shouted the doctor. "You seem to have no trouble at all. . . ."

"Oh," lamented the old man, "I have no trouble at all if I am given a chance. Trouble is I don't ever get the chance."

The whole wagon was roaring with laughter. Modche waited patiently for the S.S. men's reaction.

"O.K.," the two drunken S.S. men exclaimed. "You have

won. The restrictions on the "bucket" are removed for the rest of the journey."

On Monday morning the journey came to an abrupt stop, and the happy atmosphere created by Modche's many jokes soon disappeared. At a siding near a small station we were ordered out of the wagon and lined up five deep. There was great excitement among the guards, who were now as wild and as vicious as ever. Suddenly the secret was out. From the center wagon a body was carried out, followed by an S.S. man whose neck was heavily bandaged. The prisoner, we were told, lost his nerve after being picked out by the guard and bullied throughout the journey. When he could no longer bear the bullying he threw himself on the S.S. man and tried to tear his neck apart. The second S.S. man shot the prisoner on the spot, but not before his colleague had been severely mauled.

The injured guard was rushed to the hospital; we were given a "lecture" by the senior officer and then shoved back into the train along with the lifeless body of the murdered prisoner.

Our two guards were no longer interested in jokes. They turned on us viciously and ordered us to kneel for four hours in punishment for the crime committed in the neighboring wagon. From then on the train journey was hell. "Bucket" only once a day; talking strictly forbidden; eating only at appointed times.

As night fell again, we were thankful to God for the creation of darkness, and for the fact that people must sleep, even if they are inhuman S.S. men.

NIEDER-ORSCHEL

13

SOMEWHERE NEAR noon on the following day, Tuesday, October 31, 1944, we arrived at our destination. We did not know where we were except that we were no longer inside the Auschwitz nightmare camp, but we were not too optimistic. There might be even worse in store for us.

The train had stopped on a siding near a small railway station, and watched closely by a group of S.S. men and one *Kapo* who stood nearby, the usual unloading ceremony took place in all its brutality. This time, we had the S.S. men inside with us, and as they knocked us out of the wagon with their rifle butts, we piled on top of each other as we fell to the ground.

The first snow of the season was falling lazily on the Fatherland, and the cold was indescribable. We were beyond being insulted now, so we meekly picked ourselves up, not needing the sharp order to stand five deep to get ready for the handing-over ceremony. As at a rehearsed military parade, we stood at attention watching with fearful eyes the leading S.S. officer from our train greet his opposite number from the camp with a well-drilled *Heil Hitler*.

"Four-hundred-fifty *Haeftlinge!*" he announced smartly. "Four-forty-nine alive; one dead!"

Our new taskmaster, a middle-aged, red-faced, bowlegged *Oberschaarfuehrer,* marched along our tired and worn-out line, horsewhip in hand, to take the count. He found 449 of us standing upright, and the dead man from yesterday's train incident lying at the end of the line, quite uncovered.

"Correct!" he confirmed, and after exchanging the routine salutes and *Heil Hitlers,* he bade farewell to the parting S.S. men.

"And now," taunted one of the S.S. men leaning from the train, "now you will learn how to do some useful work—just for once in your bloody lives."

"And you," came a hidden voice, answering spontaneously from our column, "you will go to the *Ostfront* (East-Front) for a nice holiday."

The S.S. man's face reddened at the mention of the word "*Ostfront,*" but he had no time to find the cheeky *Haeftling* as the order came for us to march off.

The word "East-Front" had by now become a curse in Germany, as the fear of falling into the hands of the Russian Army haunted all the Germans, especially the S.S.

Our new camp was only a few hundred yards away from the station, and we were particularly heartened to note that it was a very small camp, about a quarter-of-a-mile square, encircling two huge factory-type buildings, and an open *Appell* ground. There were, of course, the inevitable watchtowers along the high wire fences, but when we noted with relief the absence of the ghastly, terrifying red-brick buildings—the crematoria and the white-walled gas chambers—we experienced the feelings of doomed men who are suddenly removed from the condemned cell and taken into the prison proper.

As we marched towards the camp entrance, I took a quick look at the nameplate of the station. The entire length of the platform was covered by a huge banner reading, *"Raeder muessen rollen fuer den Sieg—Unnuetze Reisen verlaengeren den Krieg!"* ("Wheels must roll for victory—unnecessary journeys prolong the war!") Under this banner I noticed some small plates apparently giving the station's name: NIEDER-OR-SCHEL. I had never heard of the place.

"What kind of factory do you think they have in this forsaken backyard here?" I whispered to Benzi.

He did not hear me. His eyes were fixed on that huge banner. It seemed to infuriate him.

"What's wrong, Benzi?" I asked.

"Here," he said angrily, "they restrict people travelling, and there they have enough trains and coal to transport little children to their deaths. The killing of Jewish children appears to them to be more important than their victory. May God never forgive them," he added bitterly.

I was alarmed to see Benzi so upset, for he had controlled himself rigidly these past few days. I hoped he was not going to break up now. No doubt he had his wife and two children in mind when he looked at the passengers on the platform awaiting the next train. I was glad when *Kapo* interrupted our thoughts and led us into our new "home."

The camp was not empty. Already a few hundred Russian, Polish, and Czech political prisoners were installed, and they were all at work when we entered. *Kapo* took us straight into the dining hall on the first floor, and we were flabbergasted when we noticed the clean tables, benches, and tin plates with spoons laid out ready for a meal.

"*Meine Herren*," *Kapo* Otto welcomed us, "you will each receive a plate of hot soup and bread, and then I shall take you to your living quarters."

This was just too fantastic to be true. We were only three days away from Auschwitz. Where was the catch?

Later, we learned that Nieder-Orschel had originally been

[129]

intended for German prisoners only, hence the location and better equipment.

We enjoyed a plate of hot *Milch Suppe,* and then went down to the barracks, to book our sleeping berths. Benzi, Baruch, Schiff, Grunwald, Gestetner, Modche Fischhof, young Walti Braun, Hugo Gross, Herlinger, Weinberger, Dr. Tauber, I, and all the other Bratislavians went into Room No. 10 to take possession of the newly-built bunks, upon which were straw and a blanket for each man.

Eager for long-awaited rest, I jumped onto the bunk, with Modche Fischhof as my immediate neighbor, with Benzi and Grunwald on the floor below. It was nearly two weeks since I had last been able to lie down properly with room to stretch my limbs. This little break was about the best thing I could have wished for inside the wires. I gave a deep and satisfying yawn.

"Would you like your morning papers now, sir?" Fischhof wisecracked from the adjoining bunk.

"No papers, and no visitors today," I riposted. "I am having a long sleep—who cares what the papers have to say?"

Benzi, in the bunk below, did not endorse my remarks. "I'd give my tomorrow's food ration for a paper," he declared. "Even a German one. Here we are in a place we've never heard of; for the past two weeks we haven't heard a thing about the war. Where are the Russians? How far are the Allies? Our lives depend on their every move. Oh, if only I had news. . . ."

But hopes of getting a paper, even in this camp, were as remote as that of getting a good rest. *Kapo* Otto with his stupid Polish *Stubendienst,* Chaskl, came marching in, ordering all of us out on to the ground for *Appell.*

On the freshly snow-covered *Appell* ground our *Ober-schaarfuehrer,* still with his horsewhip, the *Schaarfuehrer,* a tall, good-looking man, and the *Unterschaarfuehrer,* a short fellow with a vicious-looking Alsatian by his side, stood in a tight group. There were also three civilians—two in white overalls, and one in civvies. The latter was *Ingenieur* Schenk, the man who the week before in Auschwitz had picked us out for his transport in Pinkus' horrible block.

The *Oberschaarfuehrer* addressed us:

"You will work in these factories here, building wings for the *Luftwaffe's* fighter aircraft. Nobody knows you are here, and nobody knows of this factory. We demand utmost capacity work from each and every one of you. Any slacking in work is sabotage. Any misuse of raw material is sabotage. Unpermitted absenteeism from work is sabotage. And sabotage is punishable by death. Is that clear?"

"*Jawohl!*" we echoed.

Then the civilians, accompanied by the S.S., marched along the line of men asking everyone for his previous occupation. We knew that it would be fatal to admit having been in business, or a profession, as the Germans wanted manual laborers, not merchants or doctors. Everyone pretended to have been a physical worker before imprisonment.

"*Was bist Du?*" the short little *Unterschaarfuehrer* asked me sharply.

"I was a dental student," I said, remembering that at my age, and with my soft hands, I could not pretend to have been a woodchopper or bricklayer.

"He'll make a good driller!" said the man in the white overalls. He wrote my name down and asked me to stand in a corner to the left where there were already quite a number of men.

By the time *Appell* finished it was almost dark and there were about five groups of prisoners. Benzi, Grunwald, and a number of others were in a group opposite me. They were selected for *Umschulung*—retraining.

The *Unterschaarfuehrer* then announced that we would work in two shifts: one from seven in the morning to seven in the evening, and the other through the night. I was picked for the first night shift, starting the same evening, and was to go to Halle Two, which was the second hall from the camp. I was very unhappy at having been separated from my friends, and unhappier still when I saw that Benzi and the rest of them would start with the day shift. This meant that we would only meet once a week, that is, on Sundays, when work finished at four-thirty in the afternoon.

Punctually at six forty-five we were ordered out, and taken under S.S. escort into Halle Two. It was a massive tin building—the size of a football pitch, with half-finished airplane wings hanging on hoists throughout the length of the hall. The foreman, or *Meister,* as he was called, took me to a Russian prisoner saying: "You will work with him."

I looked at this tall, thirty-year-old Russian with a fat round face and a broad Mongolian nose, and he without a word put a heavy pneumatic drill into my hands and motioned me to drill a hole into the huge aluminum sheet that was swinging about in front of me. He could not speak a word of German, apart from *"Weiter machen, weiter machen,"* words which he must have picked up from the *Meister,* and I had not the slightest idea how to get the drilling needle to start turning. I tried to make myself understood by speaking to him in Czech, which after all is also a Slavic language, but he just waved me away and returned to his job.

I took an instant dislike to this coldly hostile fellow, and decided that somehow I must get myself transferred to another worker. I stood still, drill in hand.

"Why don't you work?" came the demanding voice of the *Meister.*

"I don't know how to use this drill—and I cannot make myself understood to this Russian fellow."

Meister took the drill away from me and bade me watch him carefully as he drilled a number of holes into the aluminum. I kept my eyes on *Meister* more than on the job. He was a middle-aged man, definitely not a villager. Altogether he seemed to me to be a kindly fellow. I decided to have a little chat with him.

"Thank you, *Herr Meister*, for showing me the job so patiently," I began, "but how can you expect me to concentrate on a new job after having spent three nights and two days in a stinking cattle-truck? I really do want to work, and work hard, but I cannot even keep my eyes open."

"*Ja, ja,*" he said, "there is a war on and we all have to work hard. Here, have a go yourself." He put the drill back into my hands, and I pulled the trigger and let the needle work its way into the silver aluminum.

"Good, good," he said as I finished my first hole, "you will pick it up soon—but keep the drill straight, and hold it firmly against your belly."

I went on drilling closely watched by *Meister*. When the tension was mounting in my mind, he said: "How old are you?"

"Just nineteen."

"*Ja.* I, too, have a son of your age. He is a prisoner of war somewhere in England. They treat them very rough over there. Heaven knows how he is getting on."

That was a good lead for me. I was afraid of getting into a discussion about POW treatment in England, although I would have gladly changed places there and then. But I did feel that I might at least get him to take me away from the Russian.

"I am sure, Herr *Meister*," I went on, "that since you are treating your people in your group so well, your son will also be having it easy."

"Oh, yes," he said quickly, "I never did wrong to the prisoners here. They cannot help being here, just as my son cannot help being there."

"Herr *Meister*, I am really so tired," I pleaded, "and I think I am running a temperature. Do you think you could transfer me this evening, just tonight, to an easier job?"

He looked at me, and walked away. I congratulated myself, only to know terror when he returned with an S.S. man. I thought of the *Oberschaarfuehrer's* words and wondered whether I hadn't overdone it with the *Meister*.

"This *Haeftling* has temperature. He ought to get back into the barrack."

The S.S. man, an old and small fellow, motioned me with his head to follow him, and I went back into the barrack.

The block was in complete darkness, lights had gone out soon after eight, but I could still make out Benzi's reddened face.

"Are you mad?" he protested, as I told him of my experience. "You cannot dodge work here. You are risking your neck!"

I tried to make Benzi understand that it was impossible to work with that Russian fellow as a partner, and that I had to get away. But he would not listen.

"What will you do tomorrow?" he asked.

I, too, was worried about that, but when the morning came I found that I had indeed developed a very high temperature. I could hardly keep my eyes open and my limbs and bones were aching.

I rose, together with the rest of the day shift men, at four-thirty in the morning, went into the ice-cold washroom, stripped to the waist for a wash, carefully watched by *Kapo* Otto and the *Stubendienst*, and then collected my daily ration—a sixteenth of a large black loaf, a spoonful of jam, one ounce of margarine, and half a liter of atrocious black coffee. I next joined the group for *Appell*, but as soon as this was over, I collapsed and was carried to the *Revier*, the Red Cross room which was occupied by a French and a Hungarian doctor. They took my temperature, which was near 104, and ordered me to remain in the barrack for *Blockschonung.*

I went back into the block, empty except for a few snoring night shifters, and wondered what would happen to me next.

14

BENZI TOOK one look at me when he returned from his first morning's work in Halle One, and then asked in a whisper: "What's wrong?"

I croaked about my temperature and said my throat felt as rough as an emery board. That much must have been obvious to Benzi from my hoarse voice.

"You'll feel better when the soup comes," he suggested.

I agreed. Since the five A.M. coffee—over seven hours ago—I had had no fluid.

Benzi was moving towards Dr. Tauber. The next moment the two of them were bending over me.

As he sounded my chest I thought of the well-dressed, fresh-looking Dr. Tauber who used to visit me at home. Now he was only a shabby and hungry *Haeftling* who was "appointed" that morning to sweep the huge Halle Two of the piles of aluminum dust that gathered throughout the day.

Dustman Tauber gave his diagnosis to Benzi in these words:

"The boy's throat is as red as fire. He has a high temperature. I cannot, of course, be sure how high. He has little resistance.

[136]

Cheer him up a bit and try to 'organize' an extra plate of soup for him."

Benzi had no difficulty in "collecting" a few spoonfuls of soup from everyone at the table, and I felt somewhat relieved after having had two helpings of the heavy gray mixture prepared by our Czech "chef," Josef. It contained diced vegetables, shreds of meat, and some potatoes; it was far from palatable, but at least it was hot. Benzi returned to the Halle for the afternoon shift.

On Thursday morning I managed to rise from my bunk with the rest of the men, but I was obviously too ill and too weak to join them for work.

I reported at the *Revier* again. The official French doctor disinterestedly shoved the thermometer under my arm and turned to attend to the queue who required bandages for their injured limbs. I had reached 104°, so I was granted a further day of *Blockschonung*.

"Can't I have a few aspirins?" I begged him.

Without replying, he motioned me out of the line. I had a couple of minutes with my friends before they went back to their jobs in Halle One.

"If only I could get a few aspirins I'm sure I could get this temperature down," I said anxiously to Benzi.

Benzi looked more worried than ever. "The trouble is we don't know any of the *Meisters* yet. I might pick the wrong man if I approached one by chance."

No sooner were the barracks quiet, with the day shift at work and the night shift asleep, than the *Unterschaarfuehrer*, whom we called "The Dog" because of his ever-present Alsatian, came in to check that the beds were correctly made, and to note those who were not at work.

"*Meister* in Halle Two reported you missing," he said to me sternly. "He said you dodged work on the very first night."

"*Herr Unterschaarfuehrer*," I pleaded. "*Meister* must have made a mistake. I don't belong to Halle Two. I was selected for *Umschulung*, for retraining, but have fallen ill on the first evening and have not yet been to work."

I had already planned to dodge Halle Two and to join Benzi and the rest of them in Halle One. Now seemed the best time to start my deception.

"Have you been to the *Revier?*"

"Yes, sir. I have 104° temperature. They granted me *Blockschonung.*

"*Blockschonung?*" he mocked. "That fool doctor needs replacing. You are not ill! You are a lazy bug. If you are not at work by tomorrow you will go to the *hospital!*"

He put so much stress on the word *hospital* that I had little doubt of the treatment that I would receive there.

The barrack was cold and drafty, but all I could do was lie in my bunk and pray. I had come through the hell of Auschwitz by what I thought of as a miracle. I must not now lose my chance of survival. Prayer was my only hope, and pray I did, incessantly, to the Healer of all sick.

I resolved that no matter what my condition I would rejoin the working party, so on Friday morning I told Benzi that I would join them for *Umschulung,* and begged him to smuggle me into Halle One.

After breakfast and *Appell,* during which "The Dog" made a special point of checking my presence in the working party, I went into Halle One. I considered that my chances of being recognized were remote. The German *Meisters* did not as yet know all the prisoners. We all looked too much alike—a group of shabby, dirty, "dangerous" Jews who must have spent years in prison before reaching this camp. Unobtrusively, I followed Benzi and Grunwald to their workbench, but the nearby *Meister* pulled me up immediately.

"Hey, you, who are you? You don't belong here. Where's your toolbox?"

My heart jumped. Benzi must have forgotten to tell me about the box of tools and the drawer I was supposed to keep them in. I mustered all my forces.

"But I do belong here, Herr *Meister*," I said eagerly. "I have been selected for retraining, but I fell ill on the evening of our arrival here."

The *Meister* grimly sized me up. "You don't look like too much of a worker to me. In any case, *Umschulung* finishes next Monday. There is no point in your starting now. Perhaps they will have you in Halle Two."

The mere mention of Halle Two brought to mind the fear of joining up again with that miserable Mongolian with whom I had worked on the first evening. I was sure that the *Meister*, who let me off that first evening and then hastily reported me to the S.S., would have held it against me for trying to switch jobs.

"*Herr Meister*," I argued. "I'll pick the job up quickly, and will be ready by next Monday. I am handy with tools of this kind. I have always worked on similar jobs."

"I suppose that is why they picked you for *Umschulung*, eh?" he said sardonically.

I could have bitten out my tongue at this stupid lie of mine which obviously contradicted my selection for retraining. Nevertheless, the *Meister*, who could not really care about the progress of his pupils, agreed to keep me "just for the day" and see how "I got on." He gave me a drill, a much smaller one than those used in Halle Two, told me to drill holes into two small pieces of aluminum, then use a countersink drill, and finally rivet them together with the small pneumatic riveter hammer. He showed me how it was done and then left me to carry on. Quickly I slipped the two samples which the *Meister* himself had made into my pocket and then, with the assistance of Benzi and Grunwald, slowly started on my job.

When the *Meister* came before lunch to check on my progress, I pulled out the two small pieces from my pocket, showed them, and listened with delight to his expression of admiration at the quick way I had picked up the job.

Suddenly an S.S. man appeared. In camp, the S.S. always engendered fear, and I prepared myself for the showdown when he would demand why I had switched from Halle Two to Halle One. But all the S.S. man required was half-a-dozen volunteers to unload a wagon of coal that had arrived at the station for the factory. Obviously the *Umschulung* bench was immediately chosen as being able to spare the necessary men.

I, the new boy, was the first to be selected by the *Meister*, followed by Benzi, Grunwald, young Walti Braun, and two others. Under S.S. escort we were marched to the railway station and given the task of pushing the coal-laden wagon into the siding leading to the camp.

The sight of a train just pulling in made us pause in our labors.

"How about a nice trip home?" Benzi joked to Grunwald.

"Thinking of making a break for it?" the S.S. man intervened, as if reading our thoughts.

"No," Grunwald joked. "We would not dream of it—we only travel first class."

"Smart, aren't you?" the S.S. man responded. "Well, we'll soon see how smart you all are with this load of coal. Get the wagon on the move!"

We should have been wise enough by now not to break the old rule never to speak to an S.S. man unless absolutely necessary. That S.S. man gave us a hell of a time. He beat and butted us unmercifully until the six of us finally managed to get the wagon on the move.

On reaching the end of the line we jumped onto the wagon and began to push the coal down with the shovels. At first the job was quite easy. But once we cleared the upper section, and had to heave our heavy shovels over the sides of the wagon, the strain began to tell. Benzi did his best to try and spare me as long as he possibly could, in view of my illness. But there was fourteen-year-old Walti Braun to be considered, for whom the job was equally strenuous.

The S.S. man insisted that the job had to be finished before darkness fell, and his bullying commenced afresh.

"Can we slide the doors open and let the coal roll out from the sides?" we pleaded after clearing almost half the wagon.

The S.S. man guffawed. "Not likely. You are far too lazy, that's the trouble with all you Jews. Get working."

Two more S.S. men climbed into the wagon and kicked us every time we straightened our backs. For well over two hours they kept us slaving. We were not allowed a moment's respite.

Long after darkness had fallen, our cruel task was completed and we crept back to the barracks exhausted. My hands were raw and blistered. My back appeared to be on the verge of breaking down completely, but I had sweated so much that afternoon that my temperature, and even my sore throat, had vanished.

"If I survived this afternoon," I groaned to Benzi as we rested on the bunks, "then I shall survive the whole of the war, too. Only God could make me stand up to six hours' hard shovelling after two days with a high temperature. The will to survive is all we need."

Next morning I returned to Halle One and, to my relief, was accepted with the rest of the retraining group without further challenge.

Work finished about four o'clock on Sunday afternoon, and for that day there was no night shift.

Kapo Otto came into the barracks to give us our registration numbers. Having been "transit inmates" in Auschwitz, we had not been given an Auschwitz number and therefore had no tattoo on our arms, but now that we had been settled "permanently" we were given our prison numbers. Two white strips of linen were to be sewn on the jacket and coat. For some reason we were not tattooed. My number was 95603.

Otto, who was interned because he was a Communist, and had spent ten years in prison before coming to Nieder-Orschel, was a quick-tempered man, but otherwise not too difficult to get on with. If he thought he was being disobeyed, he would blow up into an uncontrollable temper, and then his fists would fly mercilessly in every direction. Benzi was once felled by a vicious blow when Otto thought that he was contradicting his command.

On that particular Sunday afternoon, however, Otto was wearing his usual charitable smile and allowed himself to be drawn into conversation.

"*Kapo!*" Someone in our barrack asked. "How come we have such a high number? This is only a small camp."

"*Menschenskind!*" Otto shot out in surprise. "Don't you know we belong to Buchenwald? You have a Buchenwald number."

"Buchenwald?" we echoed in astonishment. "Where is Buchenwald?"

"Buchenwald is only a short train ride from here," Otto explained. "We are under Buchenwald command and indeed receive regular visits and inspections from them. Many a prisoner has been sent there for punishment. It will pay you to remember that."

Otto's disclosure was profoundly disturbing. We knew Buchenwald was almost as infamous as the dreaded Auschwitz, and the knowledge that we were within easy reach, and, indeed, under the command of this extermination camp, spelled fear and death to us all. It was then that I realized what "The Dog" meant when he warned me the previous week of a trip to the "hospital." There was a gloomy mood in the barracks.

"*Meine Herren*," Otto called out. "Don't be so upset. I have good news for you today."

We waited without much interest.

"You have permission to write a letter home once every month. Those who want to write should report to me and they will be given one sheet of paper, an envelope, and a pencil. You must, of course, not write anything about your where-abouts, the conditions here, or about your work. On the back of the envelope, as well as on the letter, you will write your name, your prison number, and the words 'Buchenwald 110.'"

Some of the prisoners, particularly the Russian, Czecho-slovakian, and Italian political prisoners, as well as the Ger-mans, received the news with great jubilation. To us Jews, however, it only served to sadden us more deeply. Write home? To whom? To what address? To the Auschwitz crematoria?

Nevertheless, most of us joined the queue outside Otto's room, waiting in turn to receive the paper and pencil. Hugo Gross, a Bratislavian, who stood in the queue in front of me, said he was going to write to his German ex-boss in Sudeten-Germany. He shrugged. "I have nothing to lose. I used to be their travelling salesman for many years, and the boss always liked me. That is, before Hitler came. I'll write to him. We will see what happens."

Not to be outdone, I wrote to a non-Jewish woman servant who had worked for our Jewish neighbors in Bratislava over thirty years. A kindly soul, I was sure she would remember me once the letter reached her.

"Dear Yanka," I wrote, "I hope that these lines will find you in good health. I'm keeping well and have many friends with me. If you could send me a little parcel of either food or cloth-ing, I would be very glad indeed. With kind regards, yours sincerely. . . ."

I addressed the letter to her at the address where we lived, for I knew that the postman would find her. The only change

I made was to write "Pressburg, Germany," instead of "Bratislava, Slovakia." I thought that they might not deliver mail to Slovakia in view of the partisan activities there.

On the following Monday, a huge new pneumatic riveting press was wheeled into Halle One and *Ingenieur* Schenk went up to *Meister* asking him to delegate his three best pupils for the machine.

Benzi, Grunwald and I were selected. We had to feed into the machine two huge sections of the plane wing which hung over the press from a hoist suspended from the ceiling. Then we had to rivet them together in accordance with the holes and marks duly prepared by the men in Halle Two. We were pleased with the job. We had the satisfaction of being together, and were able to spend the time chatting comfortably about the past, and even venture to guess on our future. It made everything much easier and more acceptable. But the infernal noise of hundreds of pneumatic drills and the banging of riveting hammers was at times deafening, so that talking was impossible. The dust from the sawn aluminum sheets clogged our throats and noses until we felt stifled.

We settled down in Nieder-Orschel as best we could. Benzi was elected *Tisch-Aeltester* (Table Elder), with the task of sharing out to the group at his table the rations of soup, portions of bread, etc.

Our one hope was that the war would not last much longer. If conditions grew no worse here, we considered we could manage to survive this camp without too many losses, despite the fact that prisoners were now beginning to collapse at every *Appell* from sheer exhaustion, or from lack of willpower to carry on the struggle. Alas! Our small moral reserves were to be strained to their utmost. *Meister* Meyer, who was put in charge of our huge pneumatic press on day shifts, proved himself to be a sadistic bully and a most dangerous anti-Semite. There could be no slacking under his ever-alert eyes, but we did our utmost to avoid giving him his eagerly awaited chance to report us to the S.S.

The grim fight for survival against time was on. Would we make it?

15

THERE APPEARED to me to be two ways of surviving these camps of death. The first was to forget or abandon all laws of decency, respect, and trust in your fellow men, and fight recklessly and ruthlessly for your own skin, irrespective of any consequences to your fellow inmates. You had to rob, steal, and "organize" for extra food and better working conditions, curry favor with your *Meisters*, and squeal on your colleagues for the price of an apple or slice of bread.

The second was to hang on to dear life by trying to find hope and courage beyond human power.

There were plenty who adopted the law of the jungle, and they became the terror of the camp. I—and many like me—could never bring myself to pick someone else's pocket while standing to attention at *Appell*, or rob him of his last piece of bread or wurst, or indulge in tricks which those who had been in the camps much longer than we appeared to accomplish so easily, and without conscience pricking them.

Some of us preferred to adopt the old and tested Jewish

method of finding hope and strength in God, and in prayer to Him. Thus, every morning and evening, fifteen or twenty of us crouched together quietly between the bunks to recite some parts of the prayers, and then go to work or to sleep, encouraged by the knowledge that the God for Whose sake we suffered was listening to our pleas.

Some laughed and mocked us. *Kapo* Otto, the faithful Communist, could cripple you for finding you at prayer; the S.S. would send you to the "cooler" for a couple of days for it, yet most of those sitting at what was called the "religious" table joined us regularly for a prayer session. There were: Benzi, the Table Elder; Baruch Stern, my former neighbor; Modche Fischhof, my "sleeping partner"; Hugo Gross, who wondered what his former Sudeten-German boss would say when he received his letter; Weinberger, the optician who was always hungry; Max Schiff, who was considered foolish for admitting having been a secretary, and yet was rewarded for his frankness by getting an office job with no night shift, with the solace of working in a warm room. Then there were old Mr. Friedman, the eldest in the camp, who escaped the death chambers after showing an S.S. man his rough hands to prove that he was still able to work; young Walti Braun, who often wet his bed at night to the disgust and annoyance of Benzi, who slept in the bunk directly under him. There were Herlinger, the pessimist; Akiba Simcha Ungar, the young rabbi whose prison number was one less than mine—95602; Gestetner, Modche Fischhof's brother-in-law; thin Mr. Herzog; Federweiss, who wanted to chisel his way out of the transport between Sered and Auschwitz; Dr. Tauber, who often repeated to me some impressive words which he heard from my late father's sermons; and, of course, Joszi Grunwald.

As winter advanced and grew colder, life became much more difficult. The midday soup ceased, and we had to spend the half-hour break inside Halle One watching the

Meisters eating their sandwiches and smoking their cigarettes. We now felt the effects of working for twelve hours without food or drink. The skin on our hands began to peel, and every tiny cut or prick became septic, and took days to heal. The evening soup became thinner and thinner, and most of us had to run four or five times every night to the toilet. The thirty-minute *Appell* in the knee-high snow froze our feet. This, and the absence of any news about the progress of the war, reduced our nerves to breaking point.

Escape was completely ruled out, not only because of the strong guard and high wire fences, but because we had no chance of replacing our striped clothing, or of obtaining money or documents to get us past the first road control into a train.

When writing the little diary in which I entered the Hebrew dates and festivals, I discovered with great delight that *Hanukkah*, the Festival of Lights, the festival on which we commemorate the recapture of the Temple from the mighty Greeks by a handful of faithful Jews, was only a few days ahead. I decided that we should light a little *Hanukkah* lamp even in Nieder-Orschel, and that this would go a long way towards restoring our morale.

Benzi was immediately consulted because he had become the most reliable and trusted person in the block. Even those at the other two tables—the "intellectuals' table," where the doctors, lawyers, dentists, architects, and businessmen ate, and the "free table," where the non-believers sat—even they came to Benzi to settle their quarrels, which were mostly about the distribution of their rations. Benzi would stand no arguments at his own table. He cut every loaf into eight portions and shared it out indiscriminately. He who complained, received the smallest portion.

"If you are dissatisfied," Benzi would shout angrily, "go and join another table, where they have scales and judges."

Nobody ever left our table.

Benzi was enthusiastic about my idea. "Yes, we should get a *Hanukkah* light burning," he said. "It will boost our morale and lighten the atmosphere. Work on a plan, but be careful."

Two problems had to be overcome: oil had to be "organized," and a place had to be found where the lighted wick would not be seen.

There was no lack of oil in the factory, but how could we smuggle even a few drops into our barrack in time for Monday evening, December 11, the first night of *Hanukkah?*

We knew, of course, that Jewish law did not compel us to risk our lives for the sake of fulfilling a commandment. But there was an urge in many of us to reveal the spirit of sacrifice implanted in our ancestors throughout the ages. We who were in such great spiritual as well as physical distress felt that a little *Hanukkah* light would warm our starving souls and inspire us with hope, faith, and courage to keep us going through this long, grim, and icy winter.

Benzi, Grunwald, Stern, Fischhof, and I were in the plot. We decided to draw lots. The first name drawn would have to steal the oil; the third would be responsible for it, and hide it until Monday evening; and the fifth would have to light it under his bunk. I was drawn fifth.

Grunwald, who was to "organize" the oil, did his part magnificently. He persuaded the hated *Meister* Meyer that his machine would work better if oiled regularly every morning, and that this could best be arranged if a small can of fine machine oil was allotted to us to be kept in our tool box. *Meister* Meyer agreed, so there was no longer the problem of having to hide it.

On Monday evening after *Appell*, everyone else sat down to his much awaited portion of tasteless but hot soup, while I busied myself under the bunk to prepare my *Menorah*. I put the oil in the empty half of a shoepolish tin, took a few threads from my thin blanket and made them into a wick. When everything was ready I hastily joined the table to eat my dinner before I invited all our friends to the *Hanukkah Light Kindling* ceremony. Suddenly, as I was eating my soup, I remembered we had forgotten about matches.

I whispered to Benzi.

"Everyone must leave a little soup," Benzi ordered his hungry table guests, and told them why.

Within five minutes, five portions of soup were exchanged in the next room for a cigarette. The cigarette was "presented" to the chef, Joseph, for lending us a box of matches without questions.

And so, as soon as dinner was over I made the three traditional blessings, and a little *Hanukkah* light flickered away slowly under my bunk. Not only my friends from the "religious" table were there with us, but also many others from the room joined us in humming the traditional *Hanukkah* songs. These songs carried us into the past. As if on a panoramic screen, we saw our homes, with our parents, brothers, sisters, wives, and children gathered round the beautiful silver candelabras, singing happily the *Maoz Tzur*. That tiny little light under my bunk set our hearts ablaze. Tears poured down our haggard cheeks. By now, every single inmate in the room sat silently on his bunk, or near mine, deeply meditating. For a moment, nothing else mattered. We were celebrating the first night of *Hanukkah* as we had done in all the years previous to our imprisonment and torture. We were a group of Jewish people fulfilling our religious duties, and dreaming of home and of bygone years.

But alas! Our dream ended much too soon.

A roar of *"Achtung"* brought our minds back to reality, and our legs to stiff attention. "The Dog"—that skinny little *Unterschaarfuehrer*—stood silently at the door, as he so often did on his surprise visits, looking anxiously for some excuse, even the slightest, to wield his dog-whip. Suddenly he sniffed as loudly as his Alsatian, and yelled:

"*Hier stinkts ja von Oehl!*" ("It stinks of oil in here.")

My heart missed a few beats as I stared down at the little *Hanukkah* light flickering away, while "The Dog" and his Alsatian began to parade along the bunks in search of the burning oil.

The *Unterschaarfuehrer* silently began his search. I did not dare bend down or stamp out the light with my shoes for fear the Alsatian would notice my movements and leap at me.

I gave a quick glance at the death-pale faces round me, and so indeed did "The Dog." Within a minute or two he would reach our row of bunks. Nothing could save us . . . but suddenly . . .

Suddenly a roar of sirens, sounding an air raid, brought "The Dog" to a stop and within seconds all lights in the entire camp were switched off from outside.

"*Fliegeralarm! Fliegeralarm!*" echoed throughout the camp! Like lightning I snuffed out the light with my shoes and following a strict camp rule, we all ran to the open ground, brushing "The Dog" contemptuously aside.

"There will be an investigation. . . . There will be an investigation," he screamed above the clatter of rushing prisoners who fled out into the *Appell* ground.

But I did not worry. In delight I grabbed my little *Menorah* and ran out with it. This was the sign, the miracle of *Hanukkah*, the recognition of our struggle against the temptations of our affliction. We had been helped by God, even in this forsaken little camp at Nieder-Orschel.

Outside, in the ice-cold, star-studded night, with the heavy drone of Allied bombers over our heads, I kept on muttering the traditional blessing to the God who wrought miracles for

His people in past days and in our own time. The bombers seemed to be spreading these words over the host of heaven.

❋   ❋   ❋   ❋   ❋   ❋   ❋

As the year 1944 drew near its end, work was considerably increased, and at our riveting machine we were ordered to complete three wings every twelve hours, instead of the previous two-and-a-half. Inmates at *Appell* collapsed every day and "The Dog" grew more and more vicious. He was particularly brutal whenever his girl friend, an ugly little round-faced girl with thick-rimmed glasses, watched him taking the *Appell* from beyond the wires. He liked to show himself off as the supreme master of all "his" prisoners, and usually one or two inmates had to suffer for it.

Meister Meyer, too, appeared to have sharpened his teeth, but while he bullied us unmercifully, our night shift *Meister*, although a younger man, showed some pity and understanding. Now and again he would allow us to go during the midnight break to the *Meisters'* dining hall and bring over whatever food, mostly soup, the *Meisters* had left. Under S.S. escort, two prisoners would walk the two hundred yards into the *Meisters'* dining room, situated outside the wires, and bring the soup over into Halle One.

Although this "extra" food was very welcome, it did not put back the strength that night shift work was taking out of my starved body. I had almost continual pain in my legs, and chilblains made it difficult for me to stand at my machine. I decided to try and have a chat with our night shift *Meister*.

"*Herr Meister*," I approached him politely one evening during the midnight break. "You know that we do our work very conscientiously, and that we have never given you reason to complain."

I stopped to await his reactions and to test his mood. He nodded.

[152]

"How many wings are we supposed to finish every shift?" I went on, as if unaware of the new regulations.

"Three."

"Right," I said, "you shall have three wings at the finish of every shift! That is, at six-thirty in the morning . . . but please don't check on our work during the night."

"What do you mean?" he snapped. "It is my job to check on you during work. That is what I am here for. Do you want me to be sent to the *Ostfront?*"

The last word was a slip of his tongue, but it was a good one for me.

"You know the *Oberschaarfuehrer* once asked me if you were kind to us—if you treated us gently during the night-shift," I continued.

"And what did you answer?" he asked nervously.

"I said that you were a proper beast and never gave us a minute's rest. The *Oberschaarfuehrer* slapped my face and said that we didn't deserve better treatment."

I watched *Meister's* face closely. He was evidently pleased with my report, and felt more at ease. "I never thought that they would go as far as all that," he said. "I never believed that they would question the prisoners about our work. . . ."

The buzzer announced the end of the break and put an end to our talk.

"Well, *Herr Meister,*" I said quickly, "will you help me as I helped you? We won't let you down or get you into trouble."

"I want to see three complete wings every morning," he said as he stamped out his cigarette, allowing me to pick one from his packet.

"*Jawohl, Herr Meister,*" I said, "and thank you for the cigarette."

From that evening we worked diligently from seven until two in the morning and finished two wings. Then we would disappear into the warm boiler house and sleep for two good hours, after which we would return to the machine and finish the third wing by the end of the night shift.

This extra break was a great help to Grunwald, Benzi, and me who worked together on that huge riveting machine. There were about seventeen hundred holes in every wing which had to be riveted together with aluminum nails of various sizes and thickness. But we did our jobs well and efficiently.

Indeed, every time we left the Halle, the sight of three completed wings filled us with a sense of guilt, for these wings were sent back to Halle Two for the electricians to fit in hundreds of little wires and contacts. From there they were transported to the body factory situated a few hundred miles away, were the wing was joined on to the plane proper, thus completing another Junker Fighter.

This thought was disturbing. For we, who could hardly await the moment of liberation, were helping with our own hands to delay that moment. We were actually assisting those who had murdered our parents and children in the most cruel and bestial manner. We were prolonging this bloody war.

"Every single plane is one step nearer to victory," the vicious *Meister* Meyer would say any day he saw us slowing down with our work.

Sometimes we would secretly laugh at him, but at other times we did not feel too sure. Perhaps he was right? What had become of the East Front? What of the Second Front? Where were the Russians and how far away were the Allies?

Shut off entirely from the outside world, and with no chance of seeing any papers except an occasional old German newspaper which reported nothing but huge German victories on land and sea, we began to fear that the war had taken a new turn, and that *Meister* Meyer's hopes for a victory might not be as fantastic as we wanted them to be.

We were, after all, helping Germany to win the war.

16

WE WENT to bed on Sunday night, December 31, 1944, completely unaware of the fact that it was New Year's Eve. Yet probably every one of those who survived Nieder-Orschel will remember that night for the rest of his life. At twelve o'clock, *Kapo* Otto burst out of his room and screamed at the top of his voice: "*Meine Herren,* it is 1945. I wish you freedom!"

In no time the entire camp population was on its feet; even the ill, the weak, and those who had long since given up all hope of survival, were screaming, dancing, or bouncing on their bunks calling out for freedom and liberation. The Russians in their rooms burst out with the "Internationale," the Poles chanted their hymn, the Hungarians theirs, and we in our room chanted the Czechoslovakian anthem.

Why did not S.S. Riot Squads enter the barracks and beat everyone into unconsciousness? They had come previously in full force for less disturbance and noise. Yet, as the minutes ticked away and the noise of the madly dancing and chanting prisoners became almost deafening, no S.S. men were to be seen or heard.

The prisoners returned to their bunks in the early hours through sheer exhaustion and fatigue. The next morning we could only draw one conclusion from the previous night's experiences, and that was that the S.S. were afraid, which clearly indicated that the situation on the war fronts was far from satisfactory for the Germans.

But it was too much to expect the S.S. to abandon their customary methods. Only a few days after that Sunday night incident, six white-faced inmates were brought from Halle Two and led through Halle One, out towards the S.S. quarters. Work stopped spontaneously in spite of the shouts and yells of the *Meisters*. Fear and terror spread through the camp.

At that evening's *Appell*, which was taken by the Commandant himself, we were given the facts.

"Six of your friends," he said sternly, passing along our columns, "have sabotaged our work and deliberately cut a number of wires in the wings! They have been caught, and will pay for their crime after appearing before an investigation committee which will meet here tomorrow.

The *Oberschaarfuehrer* concluded his speech with these words: "Every one of you who was directly or indirectly collaborating with these men will pay with his life . . . I wish you all goodnight!"

We all knew that the charge of sabotage was a fabrication. We could also well imagine the procedure which an S.S. investigation committee would adopt, and the "verdict" which they would reach. Yet the entire camp could do nothing—not even establish the whereabouts of the six arrested inmates, among whom were two Bratislavians who worked in the electrical shop in Halle Two.

The following day was a Saturday. It was very cold indeed, and snow had fallen heavily and continuously throughout the day. After work, *Schaarfuehrer* Adams ordered *Appell* to be held in the long gangway inside the barrack.

Adams, the second in command, usually took *Appell* only once or twice a week, leaving the rest to "The Dog." He puzzled us. He was a tall, handsome man of about forty, exceptionally gentle and unusually polite. We were very cautious about him. One has to be more careful with a person who is obviously on guard and masking his true personality. Rumor had it that he had been one of the worst brutes in the Concentration Camp Maidanek, in Poland, but certainly he showed no cruel streak to us in Nieder-Orschel. Was he trying to turn as the tide went against Germany? We decided that that was the case.

He took the *Appell* in his customary way, even if a little more tight-lipped than usual. As soon as he had finished, he stepped aside and nodded to *Kapo* Otto to carry on.

We stood bewildered. Why this nod to Otto, and what was there to be carried on? Why not dismiss us? Our thoughts immediately turned to the sabotage charge. Were there to be further reprisals and additional charges? Or were we to be deprived of food for a day as a collective punishment for the New Year's Eve outburst?

Otto pulled out a piece of paper from his pocket and announced that all those prisoners whose numbers were called should step aside. He called ten numbers. Then suddenly:

"Der Haeftling Nummer 95603 austretten."

It was a moment or two before I realized that the number which he had just called was my own. A cold shiver flowed through me. My heart missed a few beats as I momentarily grabbed Benzi's hand and then stepped forward to join the other nine. The rest of the men were dismissed and ordered to their barracks.

My mind had almost ceased to function. Was I to be a hostage? Was I to be accused of sabotage, or had they found out the truth about the oil and the *Hanukkah* lights? I looked at the others in the group. None of them had had anything to do with *Hanukkah*. I felt that unless Otto made a move soon, I could not stand the strain and tension much longer.

But the worst never comes when you think it will. Otto conducted us into his room, and with a smile gave each of us a little parcel. It turned out to be one of my finest moments in the camp. I raced back into the barracks to show my anxious friends the parcel which Yanka had sent me in reply to my letter.

I tore at the parcel with all the eagerness of a boy ripping open the birthday presents he cannot wait to see. There were some fancy biscuits in the shape of little animals; there was a pair of socks, one handkerchief, a packet of boiled sweets, and ah! the most valuable currency in camp, two packets of twenty cigarettes.

The sight of the yellow boxes of Lipa cigarettes reminded me of home and of Father's desk. It was Mother's daily custom to bring Father's breakfast on a tray on which there were a cup of coffee, two rolls, butter, jam, a glass of water, and a packet of Lipa cigarettes.

I thought gratefully and appreciatively of Yanka, and as it was Saturday night, I cut a few cigarettes in half and offered them to my closest friends. I decided to have some of the cigarettes myself, but to leave one complete packet for emergency purposes. Cigarettes were very valuable and would undoubtedly be useful. I spent a sleepless night however, wondering where to hide my "treasure box."

Two days later, Hugo Gross also received a parcel, from the wife of his former German employer. She sent him some clothing and food, including three rosy apples. I remember them particularly, because on consulting my handwritten calendar I found that it was on the *15th Shevat*, celebrated as the New Year of Trees, when it is traditional to eat a large variety of fruit—if possible, fifteen kinds.

At my suggestion Gross cut his three apples into tiny portions and offered them to each of us at the "religious table," giving us a chance to make the traditional blessing on fruit. It was a kindly act on Hugo's part to share his apples so unselfishly with his friends. Not surprising then, that to this very day Hugo, who now lives in Jerusalem, receives every 15th *Shevat*, a huge parcel of fruit containing at least fifteen varieties, from his camp colleague, Gestetner, who now lives in New York, in appreciation and recognition of that day in Nieder Orschel.

My plan to hold on to some cigarettes and keep them for a rainy day never materialized. Too many people knew that they were hidden in my bunk, and I began to carry them about with me. They began to lose shape and, driven by a terrific hunger, I was tempted to offer them for sale before they became unusable.

During the night shift, at the midnight break, the *Meister* delegated Grunwald and me to fetch some leftovers from the *Meisters'* kitchen, so I offered them to one of the escorting S.S. men.

"I have a packet of cigarettes for sale. Do you want them?"

"Hand them over!" he demanded in typical style.

But I was no longer afraid. "I haven't got them on me," I told him, "and I want three loaves of bread for them."

"Three loaves of bread?" he shot out. "Where do you think I'll get them from? I'll give you one loaf, no more."

I made the deal, and arranged to meet him near the door on the following evening, before the night shift went to work. I was a rich man that night: the proud owner of a whole loaf of bread—not black camp bread, but bread prepared and baked for the elite of the German army. I was glad to share it with my friends on the night shift, but particularly to offer a fair share to Benzi, my friend, who had so often given me part of his bread or soup when my hunger was unappeased by my own meager ration.

"If I were you, I would have asked for a newspaper as well as the bread," Benzi ventured, as we sat near our machines to enjoy our extra food. "We must get hold of a paper somewhere. We are completely shut off from any kind of news from the front."

"Judging by the daily air raid warnings," Grunwald suggested, "they must be getting these bombs more frequently than their bread rations. How long can they last?"

"Why the hell don't they bomb the concentration camps and the guardhouses around them?" I said bitterly, feeling for the first time no hunger at all. "If they had bombed the tracks to Auschwitz, or at least the crematoria and gas chambers, many thousands of Jews would have still been alive, and we would probably not have been here. Allied Intelligence must know of the camps, and of the large-scale murder that is taking place in them."

The buzzer interrupted our conversation.

Next day, Schiff, who worked in the office, jubilantly brought a newspaper which he had stolen from one of the architect's coat pockets. We read it in turn, and then the paper was torn up. Judging from the maps and the *Wehrmacht* reports, and taking into account German propaganda and the lies therein, we came to the conclusion that the Allies must be terribly close to crossing the German frontier, and also that the air attacks had increased considerably.

But the best piece of news on that day, the one which eased both our hearts and our consciences, was Schiff's discovery that none of the plane wings which we had made in the factory since our arrival had ever left Nieder-Orschel. Schiff discovered that they were deposited in an open field about a mile away from the camp, carefully camouflaged with tree branches and haystacks. He found out, too, that there were hundreds of plane wings in this field, and, because of transportation difficulties, there was little likelihood that they would ever reach the body factory where the planes were to be assembled.

"Out there," Schiff declared, pointing happily towards the open field, "is the cemetery of all the wings produced by us. Perhaps, one day soon, the Allies will smash them to pieces."

"If only there were a way for us to expose the cemetery to Allied aircraft," I ventured hopefully. "Perhaps we could work out a plan?"

But Benzi ruled out the idea from the start.

"It cannot be done," he insisted. "First of all, the field is snow-covered. Secondly, the S.S. would massacre the entire camp if they discovered any attempt to expose the wings."

Benzi explained that as long as the wings were in the field they were of no value, anyway. And it was certainly not worth risking precious lives for them.

To us, the knowledge that these wings, the result of three months' hard labor, were, after all, of no service to the German *Luftwaffe*, stiffened our morale. We knew now that the concentration camp Nieder-Orschel was nothing but a first-class fraud on the part of some German civilians, whose only aim was to keep the factory going in order to escape active military service. What a tragedy it was that many of our friends had lost their lives supporting this deception, and that six innocent prisoners were shut away somewhere on a charge of sabotaging wings that would never, in any case, have flown anywhere.

Yet Schiff's disclosure made us all happy for the first time since we had been rounded up at Sered, for our most painful and distressing thought was that we were actively helping to protect the people and regime which had so cruelly and mercilessly set out to slaughter and annihilate the Jewish race. The knowledge that this was not so filled us with some hope, and we felt that as long as the deception was carried on, it would help us to escape the greater peril of being transported to the nearby extermination camp, Buchenwald.

The burning question was: How long would it be before this gigantic fake was discovered?

AS THE fateful year of 1945 advanced, our supplies of raw material dwindled. Constant Allied bombing, both of factories and of railway lines, was wreaking its toll. It was just as difficult to get supplies into the camp as it was to transport the finished plane wings out of Nieder-Orschel. It was, therefore, no surprise to us when the authorities cut our food rations severely, yet insisted on keeping both shifts working round the clock.

The only difference was that when we reported for night shift at the usual hour, we were not now harried by constant calls from the *Meister* to work harder and faster. Indeed, the night shift *Meister* was no doubt relieved when he saw us retiring into our little hideout for a few hours' sleep after the midnight break. He knew as we did, that there was not enough material for the night's labor quota.

But neither the cut in our food rations, nor the fear of the closure of the factory on which our stay in Nieder-Orschel depended, troubled us half as much as the lice which affected every prisoner. This horrible plague increased in its severity

due to the change of shirts and underwear having been reduced from a fortnight to once every month. We worked,
slept, and lived in the same underwear, only taking it off
during the brief morning wash. During the day the itching was
not too bad as we moved around the Halle, but when night-
time came and we warmed our bodies under our thin blankets
and coats, the lice bites maddened us. I tried desperately not
to scratch my sore and starved body, but once I started I
could not desist, and was then driven almost insane.

Even when we received the welcome change of shirts and
pants, the relief was only momentary, for by then our coats,
jackets, and trousers, as well as blankets, were lice-ridden and
it took but a few hours for the pests to work their way onto our
bodies again.

Then came the worst blow of all. Without prior notice, 120
men, mostly from Halle Two, where work had slackened much
more than in Halle One, were lined up in the *Appell* ground
and ordered to make ready for transportation to the death
camp at Halberstadt.

My former neighbor and dear friend, Baruch Stern, and
Gestetner and a number of other personal friends of mine were
included in that ghastly transport. We tried everything within
our very limited power to get them out, but it was to no avail.
The moment of parting was sad and tragic. And yet, even in
those circumstances, when these German civilians saw their
ingenious fake coming to an early end, that cursed day shift
Meister, Meyer, pulled us up at our machine complaining that
he had received reports that we were spending half the night
asleep.

Meyer appeared to have forgotten all about the war and
that the whole Nazi edifice was now crumbling. His long-
awaited chance had finally come, and he was going to enjoy
every moment of it. Maliciously he said to us:

"So you really can make much more than the three lousy

wings which you completed every twelve hours. All these months you have deliberately slowed down production because you knew that every wing must pass through your machine before going back to Halle Two! Well, we shall hear what the Commandant has to say to all this, after this evening's *Appell*. I believe," he added with a sarcastic smile, "I believe he has a certain word for this kind of activity."

Meister Meyer turned complacently away from his three pale-faced and panic-stricken prisoners.

"This is the end," I said to Benzi as we set the machine back into motion. "He has been waiting for this moment for a very long time. We should have known that he would discover our plan."

Grunwald was all for consulting the night *Meister*. "He alone can save us from disaster," Grunwald pointed out. "If we are caught, then he is involved too. And he is the only man who can talk to Meyer."

That was, of course, quite true. But where could we find him? He only turned up for the night shift, and that followed *Appell*.

"The sleeping arrangement was my idea," I put in dismally. "I will go and talk to Meyer . . . maybe there is still some feeling in him."

"What? In that bloodthirsty Jew-baiter?" Grunwald cut in. "No amount of begging will soften him. I think threats are the only solution."

"Threaten him?" We looked at Grunwald, aghast.

"Yes, threaten him. The war is nearly over. He knows that better than us. He ought to be told that he will not survive one hour after liberation if he brings us to the gallows. He is a coward, all the Germans are cowards. He will think twice before running to the *Oberschaarfuehrer*."

Benzi gave the problem some careful thought and then de-

[165]

cided we ought to do both: plead with him first; then, if that failed, resort to threats.

We decided to wait until Meyer returned from his midday meal, and then I, the youngest and thinnest prisoner, was to be the spokesman. When I approached him after dinner, Meyer was munching some tidbit and gave me no chance to use my carefully prepared opening.

"You are afraid," he challenged in typical Bavarian style, his face grinning like an ape.

"People who have gone through Auschwitz are not easily frightened," I answered without thinking.

"Auschwitz?" he queried.

"Yes, haven't you ever heard of Auschwitz?" I went on.

Meyer looked quite disinterested. "It's a prison camp for political criminals, isn't it?"

"No," I said sharply, "it is a camp where your people commit the worst crimes ever conceived by human beings. Thousands upon thousands of men, women, children, and babies are being put to death in gas chambers. That's Auschwitz, and that's where you learn never to be afraid again."

I watched him carefully. His first reaction was important. Three lives might depend on it.

"Are you spreading British war propaganda?" he bluffed in a loud voice. "Do you know that you can swing for this kind of talk?"

Though I was quaking I managed to appear calm.

"No, *Herr Meister*," I said quietly. "These are not lies. I lost my parents and my sister and her children in these gas chambers. Gottlieb—that's Benzi—lost his wife and two children there, too. That is the truth, the tragic truth. And as for swinging—well, you have already sentenced us to death this morning. What does it matter what we swing for?"

"But *Ingenieur* Schenk was in Auschwitz. He never said anything of the kind," Meyer said, somewhat quieter.

"*Herr Meister,* do you really think they would have taken Schenk on a sight-seeing tour into the gas chambers and crematoria? Look around this huge Halle and ask anyone and everyone about Auschwitz. Ask them how they got there and whom they left there."

"But it's my duty to report you." Meyer suddenly turned official.

"Would it be human to hang three hungry and worn-out men for the crime of spending a few minutes resting? We only rested so that we could get sufficient strength to carry on with our job and get the three wings ready. Can't you understand that?"

"I cannot alter the rules. I must report you."

"*Herr Meister,* if you send the three of us to death, you will be guilty of murder. There will be a day of reckoning, whether I am here to witness it or not."

Meyer's nose quivered like a jelly; he bit his lips nervously. I knew that the call of the buzzer would part us within seconds and decided to hammer away like a boxer who has his opponent pinned to the ropes.

"There are hundreds of prisoners in this camp. Some are bound to survive these next few weeks. *Herr Meister,* it is just a matter of weeks before we are freed by the advancing troops. Save three innocent lives . . . to save yourself."

The buzzer went. Meyer did say something in reply but I did not hear it. The strain and tension, the bargaining with a murderer, were too much for me. I passed out at the sound of the buzzer and remember nothing further.

"You did well," Benzi whispered as he leaned over me on a bunk in the *Revier.*

Good old Benzi. He had cut his finger deliberately to get an excuse to visit me in the *Revier,* and to tell me that Meyer promised to keep his mouth shut.

"He said he would forget about our sleeping during the

night," Benzi said happily, and added, "but I wonder if he would have changed his mind if you had not passed out. He did show some sort of pity when they carried you out on a stretcher."

But I did not trust Meyer. He was too much of a Nazi beast to remain quiescent for long. I was right. The next morning, as we reported for work, Meyer said that we would have to work an extra three hours every day to make up for lost time.

We accepted this lesser punishment gladly. The knowledge which I gained from the doctor in the *Revier* that our friend, Akiba Simcha Ungar, the young rabbi from Bratislava, was dying, temporarily banished thoughts of Meyer and his punishment.

The French doctor, though usually strict and cold, appeared to have taken a liking to Ungar and allowed us to remain with him until his end.

Ungar remained conscious until his very last minute. We tried to make his passing easier, and assured him that he would soon be well again, and that we would all be free men very shortly. But he dismissed us with a wave of his deathly pale and skinny arm.

"It's too late. . . . It's too late," he lamented in a whisper. "Oh, I so much wanted to live and see the coming of the Messiah."

We chanted the traditional *Shema* as Akiba Simcha Ungar closed his eyes for the last time.

In my diary I made a note of his death, on the sixth *Adar*—February 18, 1945. Poor Ungar, they left his body in the washroom for well over a week before finally transporting it with, alas, a number of additional victims for cremation at Buchenwald.

Despite the changing war situation, the S.S. did not like the sight of prisoners idling in the Halles during working hours. Nor, indeed, did the German civilians enjoy the quietness. The deafening noise of hundreds of pneumatic drills and hammers banging and piercing the huge aluminum sheets was now a matter of the past and they dreaded the future. Only isolated activity was heard from the various workshops inside the Halle.

The *Meisters,* too, feared an early transportation to the crumbling German battlefields, and as for us, we dreaded the thought of transportation to some extermination camp.

But again, the knowledge of the early approach of the *Purim* and Passover festivals infused us with some hope and courage.

I approached Schiff again, asking him to "organize" some more paper from the office so that in addition to the Jewish calendar I would be able to write the *Haggadah* and finish it in time for Passover. Schiff obliged with some discarded odd pieces of paper, most of which bore on the back architectural drawings of fighter aircraft.

Each day, upon returning from an almost workless night shift, I spent an hour on my *Haggadah.* Writing from memory the story of the Exodus of the Jews from Egypt was a worthwhile task. It helped to keep my mind off our terrible tragedy and worries about the future. Even during working hours I tried to direct my attention to passages of the *Haggadah* that required writing. Happy memories were brought back to my mind of my childhood, and of the *Seder Nights* at home, when I sat at our table listening excitedly and attentively to Father's recital of the *Haggadah* which he always did so beautifully and inspiringly.

Indeed, this work served as a source of great courage and hope for me. It was a reminder that our people have gone through many difficult and tragic experiences in our long history, and have been freed each time, by the will of God, from bondage and slavery. How wise, I thought, of our great rabbis of the past to command that the stories of *Purim* and *Pesach* be repeated every year and thus remain alive among the Jewish people. Where would we have gained the courage and strength to survive all our experiences of bestial cruelty, were it not for our great and historic past?

Yes, I felt that Passover ought to be celebrated in the camp, and not just by reciting the *Haggadah*, but also by eating the traditional matzos.

I went to a foreman who worked on the tool bench, a quiet and kindly little man who occasionally dropped a small sandwich near my machine for me to pick up.

"*Herr Vorarbeiter*," I said, "I want to ask you a very great favor."

"What is it?" he said, looking surprised.

"Oh, nothing incriminating," I assured him hastily. "I want to beg you to bring me half a pound of plain flour which I require most urgently."

"Flour? What the devil do you want that for? Birthday cake?" he added facetiously.

"I require it for a purely religious purpose," I explained, "and nobody will ever find out that it came from you. You know there is no one else I can turn to."

He looked cautious. "Things are hard nowadays, the guards are strict in their inspections, and the atmosphere is tense. I can't promise."

He spoke no more than the truth. On top of the lack of raw material and transportation difficulties, ever-increasing air raid alarms reduced our working time to a few hours per shift. When work did resume, frequent power cuts would stop us again. It was obvious that within a matter of weeks, or possibly days, great changes would overtake us. The factory would have to close, and we might either be liberated in the nick of time or transported elsewhere. At the back of our minds we hoped that we would still be at Nieder-Orschel when the first American tank bulldozed its way into the village.

There were joy and laughter throughout the camp when one

[170]

bright Sunday morning, during an air raid, an Allied fighter came down in a whistling dive from a cloudless sky and shot one of the guards out of his watchtower.

Within minutes of the incident, as was to be expected, we were summoned out for a special *Appell*. They were all there: "The Dog," and his Alsatian, *Schaarfuehrer* Adams, who we heard had ordered the camp tailor to make him a civilian suit, and the Commandant, the red-faced *Oberschaarfuehrer*.

"Wipe those grins off your faces," the Commandant yelled as he ordered us to attention. "Even if your friends the Russians have made some little headway on the front, and even if they have managed to pierce our lines temporarily, I want you to know something . . . We are still here. We have managed to deal with millions of Jews. We shall deal with you, too. You might as well know right here and now that your hour will never come. DISMISSED!"

How well the *Oberschaarfuehrer* managed to wipe the grin off our faces. We returned into the barracks on that Sunday afternoon sunken, devastated, and completely demoralized. Prisoners sat in groups of three or four at the table, or on their lice-ridden bunks, carefully digesting the Commandant's words.

"It can only mean one thing," I said to Benzi, as we sat on our bunks. "They have plans to finish us all, should they have to evacuate."

Benzi looked worried as he advised: "We must surely keep our heads if we want to see liberation."

"Well, what do you suggest?" Grunwald cut in bitterly. "Do we sit here and wait for the machine guns to mow us down?"

Benzi raised his voice. "What do *you* suggest—that we storm the electric wire? Or go out and buy guns and revolvers?"

Others joined us in the conversation. "We can 'organize' tools, and arm ourselves with knives, daggers, hammers, and

[171]

spanners," Fischhof declared. "We can even make long spears from the waste metal. All we need is the proper team, working together."

"It is quite possible," Benzi speculated, "that the Commandant envied our pleasure at seeing an S.S. man shot down and decided to frighten the life out of us. It is highly improbable that he would warn us in advance that we are to be shot. If such a plan really existed, it must have been top secret."

"Yes," agreed Grunwald, "but it is equally possible that the Commandant, in his fury, lost control of his tongue and let the cat out of the bag. We would be fools to treat his warning as an empty threat."

Others thought likewise, and Benzi decided to contact some of the other room elders and discuss the provision of homemade arms. But we had little hope in the venture. As Benzi said wisely: "Nothing short of a miracle could help us succeed in overpowering these bastards."

18

WHILE WE were talking much and doing little about the provision of arms, others took more drastic steps. Only a few days after the Commandant's warning, there was panic at *Appell*. Two prisoners were missing. "The Dog," who took the *Appell*, hastily summoned the *Oberschaarfuehrer*.

Raving like a madman, the Commandant cleared everybody from the camp. Even the cook, doctors, patients, and stokers were ordered out for *Appell*. He counted and recounted us in fury.

"Idiots!" he burst out madly. "How far do they think they will get?"

The Commandant obviously feared the reaction of his own superiors. "We will catch them," he yelled frantically. "We will have them within a few hours."

He left us standing on the *Appell* ground well into the early hours of the morning, while he and his men searched every inch of the entire camp. After a very brief rest, we were out at *Appell* again and then off to work.

In the middle of the afternoon, the buzzer sounded unexpectedly and we all ceased work. The two huge doors of Halle One were opened wide and the two escaped prisoners, both Russians, were marched in handcuffed, surrounded by a dozen S.S. men bearing guns.

It was a pathetic sight. The *Oberschaarfuehrer* halted his men in the center of the Halle to make a statement:

"These two fools have exactly three more hours to live! Nothing can save them! Anyone here thinking of making a break will meet precisely the same fate. There is no escape for any of you. Not now, and not ever."

The escorting S.S. dug their rifles into the prisoners' backs, motioning them forward. They were yet to be paraded before the men in Halle Two and in the barracks. The Commandant ordered us to "carry on" with our jobs.

But no one moved. These two poor prisoners were as good as dead. As they filed out of the Halle, we pulled off our caps and stood in respectful silence.

There was no longer any doubt in our minds as to the earnestness of the Commandant's threats. That night, Benzi and the other room elders got down to some serious work on a program of opposition.

Meanwhile, work ceased completely. Not only was there no more raw material, but even the tool shop ran out of drills and spare parts.

On Saturday morning the civilians collected their personal belongings. We were pleased to see the back of *Meister* Meyer and many of his colleagues. In the rush the friendly *Vorarbeiter* sidled up to me as I did the final cleaning of my machine.

He pushed a small bag of flour into my pocket and whispered: "We shan't be coming here any more. I brought you the flour and good luck to you."

"If we are to get any matzos," I said hastily to Benzi, "it must be done this evening immediately after the termination of the *Sabbath*, otherwise we shall have no fire to bake it on."

And indeed, at the end of the *Sabbath*, Grunwald, Fischhof, and I sneaked out of the barrack and into the smithy's workshop. Fischhof worked desperately at the bellows to liven the dying embers, Grunwald worked hastily on the dough, while I cleaned up a dirty tin plate to serve as a platter.

Within half an hour three tiny little round matzos were taking shape and color, accompanied by our happy murmur that these matzos were being prepared for the sake of God and His Commandments.

Nothing as soothing and as satisfying as the knowledge that even in this Godforsaken death camp—in this dirty little backyard of humanity, where the value of a cigarette was greater than that of a life—that even here, three little matzos had been baked in preparation for the forthcoming Passover Festival.

There were tears in the eyes of every one of the eighty inmates in Room Ten, when, after nightfall on Wednesday, March 28, 1945, I opened my little handwritten *Haggadah*, lifted up the three little matzos, and recited the first chapter, beginning with the familiar opening words: "This is the bread of affliction which our forefathers ate in the land of Egypt! Let all who are hungry come and eat, let all needy come and feast with us! This year we are here, next year may we be in Jerusalem. This year we are slaves, next year we shall be free men!"

There was no longer a "religious table" and a "free table" in Room Ten. Everyone was at our table. Rabbi Domany, a little old man from Hungary who lived in the next room, was asked to sit at the head of the table and conduct the *Seder*. I read the passages from the *Haggadah* as loud as I dared, and the rest followed in a whisper.

Then, raising up a rusty cup of black coffee which he had saved from the morning in place of the traditional glass of red wine, Rabbi Domany called out in a tear-choked voice the words of the *Haggadah:* "And it is this promise which has

[175]

stood by our ancestors and by us. For it was not just one person who rose up against us to destroy, but in every generation men rise against us to destroy us. But the Holy One, blessed be He, delivers us from their hand."

How true were these words on that evening: how apt and how meaningful were they, as we sat on that quiet and very solemn evening, eating crumbs of matzos in an atmosphere of true Jewish faith and devotion.

Never before have so many men at one and the same time been so overawed in their trust of Almighty God as on that evening in Room Ten at Nieder-Orschel; never before was there such a truly solemn *Seder* service; never before was there such longing for God and His protective arm.

The verses of the *Haggadah* were apt, but in a different way the very words "Jewish Exodus" became alive again on that Passover week; for on the night of Sunday, April 1, 1945— Easter Sunday—a detachment of S.S. stormed into the barracks, driving us out of our bunks and onto the dark *Appell* ground.

Panic overtook us as screaming S.S. men with wild Alsatians cleared the barracks in a matter of minutes. Before I left, I managed to grab hold of my little *Haggadah* which I had faithfully promised to treasure until the end of my days.

Once outside, I ran to Benzi, and clasped his hand tightly. "This is the end," I cried. "I may as well meet it with my hand gripped in yours."

Benzi, always optimistic, remained silent. His plan, and that of his colleagues, had failed miserably as everyone was beaten out of the barracks, leaving the few "arms" behind in the bunks and under the straw.

Nobody expected the "call" to be so sudden and so quick. None of the S.S. men was familiar to us. When and from where had they all come?

[176]

Some prisoners wept in their terror, some prayed, and others fainted from shock and panic, as the entire S.S. population of the camp encircled us, their machine guns mounted on both sides of the *Appell* ground.

There was no need for the *Oberschaarfuehrer* to order us to be silent. No one spoke on that moonlit night. The tension was unbearable.

"We are leaving this camp tonight for another destination," the Commandant announced. "Before leaving, you will each receive a loaf of bread and whatever other food we have in store. From the moment we pass the gates, strictest order will prevail. Anyone leaving the column will be shot without warning. There can be no escape! Never . . . !"

A deep sigh came forth from the hushed crowd, as the *Oberschaarfuehrer* concluded his words.

But not for long. Some argued that they would not kill us here, in the center of a populated village: they would take us out into the fields and finish us off there.

"But why the bread and rations?" the ever-present ray of hope made itself heard.

"Camouflage . . . deception," answered the fear within us. Within an hour Camp Nieder-Orschel was quiet and deserted.

❊   ❊   ❊   ❊   ❊   ❊   ❊

As we marched out of the deserted and blacked-out streets of Nieder-Orschel, we passed the "cemetery" where all the hundreds of unused wings which we had built in this dreaded camp were deposited.

The sight of them did much to improve our morale and put fresh hope and courage into us. True, the chances of survival were now more slender than ever; the malicious *Oberschaarfuehrer* had never stopped reassuring us that our hour of deliverance would never come. And it was true that we might be stopped at any moment, and that it would take but a few minutes for these trained killers to riddle our attenuated and starved bodies with their bullets.

All this we knew. Yet no one will ever be able to measure up the amount of hope and courage that exists in a dying man. We felt that above us there was a great and mighty Power Who was now bringing the Third Reich to a final and devastating end. We knew that He also had the ways and means to rescue us from any evil plan that our captors might be preparing for us.

This, we felt, was going to be the Battle of Life. Life, freedom, and liberation were pursuing us. Death, destruction and suffering were facing us.

All that had happened since my family and I had been driven into Sered was about to be resolved.

The Hour was surely coming nearer. Whose would it be?

BUCHENWALD AND LIBERATION

19

BY NOW, the faces and varying moods of the camp S.S. guards were so familiar to us that they were part of our lives. We probably knew them and their idiosyncrasies better than they knew themselves, for we were watching, watching and waiting, all the time. We could spot a new face within a second, and the word went round like wildfire. But, accompanying us on the road were so many of these new faces and figures that we were confused and puzzled.

They were in our thoughts as we marched four abreast, with one S.S. man with a rifle to every ten lines. Behind our dismal column followed a whole line of S.S. men walking five abreast; they were, in their turn, followed by a horse-drawn cart which was loaded with S.S. provisions. The S.S. took turns riding on this cart.

Our fears grew with each mile. One of the terrors of prison life was the policy of secrecy. Whether you were to go to your doom or to your salvation, no word was uttered.

At first the brisk walk on this fine spring night was a tonic. It was months since we had exercised our limbs properly. Our maximum walk had been but the few yards leading from the barracks to the Halle.

Small wonder that the tonic soon became an ordeal: we were so unfit. But there was no stopping that night. Ruthlessly the guards pushed us on, and distressed though we were, we followed their commands in silent obedience.

An S.S. *Unterschaarfuehrer* cycled ahead of the column to study the road signs and road conditions, and every so often returned with his report to the Commandant. What was in store for us? Where was our destination? The only thing we knew was that we were being deliberately taken along narrow, deserted country roads, and that our captors were at pains to avoid roads leading into the larger cities. What could that mean, except another death camp?

Shortly before daybreak we were given our first rest. The S.S. pointed to a narrow stretch of land alongside the road and we took it that we could lie down. The guards posted themselves around us, but we paid little attention to them, for in the cold chill of dawn we fell asleep almost instantly.

Waking damp and shivering—for the dew-laden grass had soaked us through our scanty clothes—we found we had only slept for an hour, and the S.S. men were ordering us on our feet again. A few rifle shots into the air made us jump into line within a couple of seconds. And who in the history of mankind more enjoyed pulling a rifle trigger than Hitler's beasts?

Thus our second day's march began, heralded by the first of the frequent air attacks which were to accompany our forced journey. Never had we welcomed aircraft before. Now, we looked joyously into the blue sky, revelling at the roar of fast fighter aircraft coming up from our rear.

"Throw yourselves down!" ordered the S.S. wildly, but for once we were reluctant to obey orders.

The Commandant was quick to notice our reaction.

"You bloody fools!" he screamed at the top of his voice. "Do you think that those up there can recognize you as prisoners? To them you will look like retreating troops. They'll wipe you out mercilessly as they always do. They know no pity."

We soon cleared the road, pondering over the Commandant's use of the word "pity." History's greatest savages, human beasts who had set out to annihilate the entire Jewish race, and millions of others, were now talking of "mercy" and "pity"!

The fighter aircraft dived in formation and riddled the roads with machine-gun fire. How were the mighty fallen! We watched the white-faced S.S. guards with their trembling lips. Their Bren guns or even their rifles could have raked those low-flying aircraft, yet they were too scared to pull the trigger. All they could do was press their steel helmets tightly on their heads and hug the ground.

The moment the aircraft zoomed off, they were the old and vicious Master Race again.

"March slowly!" whispered a voice from the line ahead. "Pass the message along."

"March slowly," I repeated to the man behind me. "Pass the message on."

"Quite right," said Grunwald. "We shall not be able to last long at this pace. We must conserve our energy, now more than ever."

"Be in no hurry to get ahead," Benzi added. "We face nothing but evil. We want the rear to catch up with us."

But how, I wondered, should we ever be saved by the Allies coming from behind? Wouldn't we finish by being in the center of the battlefield?

"Benzi," I ventured, "we're finished. Either we shall be blown to bits by cannon fire and machine guns from the American lines, or be mowed down by the retreating Germans. The bridge dividing us from the Allies cannot collapse without drowning us in the process."

Benzi was optimistic. "Who says there is only a front and a rear? For all we know we may already be encircled by the Allies. The S.S. will be far too busy saving their own skins to bother about us. But we must hope that the attack will come soon. Only speedy action, a surprise attack, can spoil whatever plans the Nazis have prepared."

We had munched constantly at the loaf of bread in our pockets, and by the end of the second day's march our rations had given out. The S.S. removed a few sacks of lump sugar from the wagon driving behind us, gave each of the prisoners three lumps, stating that this was the last ration we would receive until we arrived at our destination.

On the third day we began to snatch the sugar beet from passing fields and carts. For the first few bites they tasted like manna, for no raw vegetables had passed our lips since we had arrived at Sered, but the aftereffects were dreadful. Our throats were raw and burning, and we had a ravaging thirst.

Water? We could as well have asked for champagne. Not before the end of our third day of marching, when we were ordered into a farmyard, and housed in sheds and stables together with the animals, did we obtain our first drink.

During the night we heard heavy shells and cannon fire in the distance, and we knew with great joy that we would be liberated in a matter of hours—if only we could hold out in the farmhouse.

"We must stay here. We must . . ." Benzi declared.

But how could we defy our S.S. guards?

We held a quick conference presided over by Benzi, who with two other senior prisoners, was delegated to approach the Commandant. The delegation was to offer him an alibi after the war if he would allow us to remain in the farmhouse, and hand us over to the liberating troops without opposition.

We held our breath while the delegation was away. When they returned they brought dubious news.

"The Commandant is ready to agree—but he is afraid of his troops," reported the delegation. "If we can obtain the agreement of every individual S.S. man, he will not object."

Alas! nothing came of that effort.

The following morning in dismal silence, we lined up on the road again. Five prisoners were missing! We were shocked, for none of us had been aware of any break for freedom.

The Commandant was furious. Cursing us roundly, he searched every inch of the farm and left us standing until nightfall. But he did not turn up the men.

On that evening, April 4, 1945, the night of the Seventh Day of Passover, a heavy storm broke over us. Thunder, lightning, hail, and heavy rain beat down on us mercilessly. Within minutes we were soaked to the skin. But we had to march on. The muddy roads made going heavy and, in places, almost impossible. Our guards clubbed us with their rifle butts indiscriminately to hurry us on.

Suddenly, Benzi, our greatest hope, collapsed. Grunwald and I picked him up and pleaded with the S.S. men to grant us two minutes' rest. They would not hear of it, so we grabbed Benzi by the arms and literally dragged him along with us.

He was in great agony. A recurrence of his hernia had gripped him. We recalled Mengele in Auschwitz stopping Benzi and asking him whether he had suffered from hernia.

After an hour of indescribable distress, Benzi pleaded with us to drop him and leave him to his fate. We knew only too well that the line of S.S. marching at the rear would riddle his body with bullets once he was helpless. So near the end of our travails, how could we desert Benzi? We drew upon our reserves of strength and dragged him along for the remainder of that never-to-be-forgotten evening.

Well past midnight our column was halted. There arose shouts and quarrels among the S.S., and we gathered that one of their observers had mistaken a turning, so that we were marching in the wrong direction.

Screamed orders for an about-face confused everyone, and we spent the remainder of the night marching back to within a mile of the farmhouse.

Then at the break of dawn, we heard shots at the head of our column. For a moment we thought that we might have clashed with an Allied Patrol. But no. . . .

As we marched on, we found the dead bodies of the five prisoners who had previously escaped at the farmhouse. They had walked straight into the hands of the scout who rode ahead of the column.

On the fifth day of our march, we reached a brick factory which had been previously inhabited by prisoners, and was surrounded by barbed wire. We were ordered inside, and the S.S. stayed beyond the wire, menacing us with their rifles.

But we had no intention of escaping. Instead, we explored the kitchen, where we found heaps of potatoes. Within minutes, it seemed, tiny campfires were twinkling all over the place, and hot potatoes were being served. Once more we cherished the hope that it would be here, in this place, that we would reach our hour of liberation. To support our hopes the welcome rattle of machine-gun fire from the nearby front was heard quite frequently.

While we were eating our roast potatoes, some of the more venturesome prisoners had broken into the factory office, and there they had come across a radio set. They had managed to tune in to London, and from the news broadcast there, they discovered the exact position of the front.

The news filled us with fresh hope.

There followed a quick conference. Encouraged by the news, and comforted by our hot meal and by the realization that the Allies could be but a few miles from us, we decided to remain inside the factory. Plans were hurriedly made to barricade ourselves inside one of the blocks, but once again we were foiled. Our movements must have been seen by one of the guards, for a few minutes before nightfall we were ordered back on the road again.

Hope and despair! Despair and hope! So it went on, taking its toll of our ebbing vitality.

Our march on this night was torturously slow. Every now and again we had to vacate the road to allow a continuous flow of retreating German armored columns containing tanks, panzers, armored cars, and lorry loads of troops, free passage. Daybreak found us still marching; but then, once again, we were shut in a farmhouse. It was becoming increasingly obvious that it was too risky for our captors to put us on the road during the daylight because of the ever-increasing air attacks that were taking place.

An hour before nightfall we were lined up again. This time thirty or more prisoners were missing. The Commandant and his troops were more furious than ever. But now they had no time to make a search. Instead they fired viciously and sporadically into the stacks of hay in the surrounding fields. If they noticed the slightest movement they set the hay alight, riddling any escapee with bullets.

I shall never know how many prisoners escaped, or how many died there that night. I shall also never forget one of the worst sights of my dreadful experiences: that of prisoners crawling out of the hay, hands held high over their heads, only to be mowed down by the guards surrounding them.

The column moved on.

After a week-end of solid marching, we were reduced to a column of slow-moving skeletons. Every so often prisoners dropped out, unable to respond even to the kicking and butting of the guards, and asked for a bullet of mercy to end their plight. This, the five S.S. men making up the rear of the column were only too glad to give.

Most of us who were left were by now walking on bare feet; others had but a few shreds of leather left to protect them. At the first sound of buzzing aircraft, we hurled ourselves into ditches and ate the raw grass just like grazing animals.

On Monday, April 9, 1945, we rested in a barn again. We picked the tall sheaves, rubbed them between our sore and skinless hands until the corn fell out, and then stuffed the barley into our mouths. We were too weak to take any notice of the repeated S.S. orders to get ready for the march again, and remained in the barn throughout Tuesday. Then, before nightfall, our guards lined up in formation and charged into the barn like a riot squad storming a crowd of demonstrators. We could not withstand their fury, and weak though we were, they got us out on the road again.

We marched lifelessly and automatically, dragging our legs up a steep hill into a thick forest. My heart sank.

"This is our end!" came the echo from all parts of the column as the S.S. suddenly halted us in the center of the pitch-dark forest. "Here they will mow us down and then escape before the Allies catch up with them."

Suddenly we were blinded by huge searchlights coming at us from all directions, trapping us in a spider's web of dazzling beams.

The entire territory was lit up as though it were day, and we saw that we were standing outside a huge and frightening-looking camp. Enormous gates were flung open, as an S.S. man shouted from the watchtower above the entrance: *"Noch ein haufen Dreck."*

The next thing we knew was that scores of S.S. men with wild Alsatians streamed out of the camp, flanked us on each side, and hustled us in.

On Tuesday evening, April 10, 1945, Buchenwald had closed its gates behind us. All hopes were gone. We could no longer care what befell us. We had suffered everything. There was

no more they could do to us. Even death would be faced in-
differently.

❋   ❋   ❋   ❋   ❋   ❋   ❋

The reception was almost the same as that in Auschwitz.
There were the "traditional" shouts and yells, the beating and
kicking of the newly-arrived prisoners. Indeed the whole well-
rehearsed, unnerving ceremony was repeated, only at twice
the speed: there was no longer the time for them to subject
us to the cruel hot-cold bath, much as our lice-ridden bodies
might have benefited by it.

No, just a quick *Appell,* and we were led into a pitch-dark
block. There we quickly invaded the first row of bunks and
squeezed ourselves on to them as tightly as sardines. Our end
might be near, but nature must be obeyed. We fell asleep immediately, exhausted from the trials of the past ten days, and
it was not until morning that we awoke to the ironic realization
that the entire block was empty, and we could have relaxed
and slept comfortably in any of the adjoining bunks.

With morning came fresh despair and fresh hope. . . . But
what was going to happen to us now?

After a three-hour *Appell,* we got into conversation with
some of the other prisoners, from whom we learned that Buchenwald itself was in the process of being evacuated.

"Thousands of people are being marched away every day to
Dachau."

"Dachau?" we echoed in surprise. "But that's about five
hundred kilometers away. How can anyone survive it?"

"You can't," they said, their gaunt faces emotionless.

And indeed, the awful news trickled through to us that about
one in three or four hundred was expected to survive this
dreadful march; the rest would die on the roads from starva-
tion, exhaustion, or bullets.

"There is only one hope," said a little Polish Jew. "Smuggle

[189]

yourselves into the Czech barracks, and get hold of a red triangle for your lapels like mine," he said, pointing to his lapel.

"But how will that help?" we asked.

He said that the Czechs, Germans, Poles, and Russians were not yet under evacuation orders. So far only the Jews were being moved.

It seemed good advice, so we hurried to the barracks to fetch our coats and to try and find the nearest Czech block. We got no further. There was a sudden shouting and our block was surrounded. We were confined to barracks.

"*Juden hierbleiben—Alle andere austretten!*" the *Kapo* ordered.

Many made desperate efforts to join the Russians and Germans of Nieder-Orschel, who were now filing out in a single line past a posse of S.S. at the door. Only two or three succeeded. The others were flung back into the barracks with bleeding heads and injured limbs. The doors were shut on us again.

By now, we all had bowed our heads to the inevitable: the Nazis did not intend that we should live to see their downfall.

Bawling guards dragged us from our apathy. We were lined up, five deep, and at two o'clock were marched under strict guard to the *Appell* ground, where we joined an enormous column of thousands of Jews.

Where now? What now?

To our surprise, rations were handed out there and then. We were given two ounces of artificial honey, two ounces of wurst, and a few stone-hard dog biscuits. And then we must have waited for a full hour before a column of heavily armed S.S. men marched in, took up positions on either side of us, and stood at attention. It was now a matter of seconds for the order to be given and the gates to be opened once more to allow the death-destined Jews to leave.

I felt that I could not last even a few more hours. I aban-

[190]

doned my overcoat, since I had not the strength to carry it: my legs were in no condition to hold up even my skinny carcass.

Then, suddenly, sirens wailed throughout the camp. As in a flash, the mass of men began running in all directions, taking no notice of guards and *Kapos*.

But there were no aircraft. Instead, cannon shells and artillery fire exploded around the entire camp. The S.S., all of them, ignored us and ran towards the main gates. Left unguarded we took refuge inside the block.

"Down!" shouted the inmates inside the barrack. "Down on the floor."

Bullets and shells screamed past our windows and pinged on the barrack roof.

"Prepare for your death," screamed a half-mad, pale-faced German prisoner, rising from the ground. "The entire camp is mined. We shall blow up as soon as the S.S. are at a safe distance. Prepare for your death! Prepare . . ."

Someone got up and felled the berserk prisoner with one blow. There was silence. Not a whisper could be heard inside the entire barrack, only the heavy shooting and exploding shells outside.

As in Auschwitz I raked my brain desperately in an effort to remember some prayer which I might recite before meeting my end. But my brain, like my body, had ceased to function. I just managed to murmur the few words of the *Shema Yisrael,* the prayer which my mother had taught me, repeating it louder and louder as if trying to outshout the noise around me. Soon, others began to pray or cry aloud until we became a mass of screaming men, each lying on his stomach, face down.

Then, emotion spent, we lapsed into uneasy silence. The minutes ticked away slowly, and the tension grew unbearable. Life and Death were having a fight outside, with us as the winner's prize. Would the camp blow up, or would the Allies manage to get in first?

I could bear it no longer. Freeing myself from Benzi's grip, I crawled slowly towards the small barrack window. Carefully I raised my head. The first thing I noticed were the empty and deserted watchtowers. The machine guns were still threateningly pointing towards us, but there was no one there to pull the triggers. Then my ears picked up an unrecognized rumble. Directing my eyes towards the main gates, I saw through thick clouds of dust and sand, a column of tanks rolling past the entrance. Their color was light brown, and a white star was painted on their sides.

"The Americans!" I screamed madly. "The Americans!"

At that very moment a white flag moved its way up a thin mast on the main front building. . . .

"A white flag!" I cried aloud. "Surrender!"

There was a mad scramble for the window. Some prisoners, afraid that one white flag would not be enough, tore their shirts off, and waved the white linen out the window.

And so the hour had come after all those terrible years. For us, just in the nick of time: for some, minutes, or perhaps seconds too late, for even as deliverance came, there were prisoners dying and dead.

"We are free, we are free!" chanted the German political prisoners jubilantly. "Free! Free!"

"Home! Home! Home!" cried the Czechs, dancing and kissing in jubilation.

We, the Jews, sank down on the floor again. No happy hopes of reunion for us. Instead, tears—big, heavy, and salty tears—stored away from the moment of our arrival in Auschwitz, forced their way out of our eyes and down our sunken cheeks. Only now did we have time to think of our dear ones who had perished in Auschwitz, and who were no longer here to see the hour of liberation and join with us in what could have been the happiest day of our lives.

Home? . . . Home! What a travesty. What was home? A place where nobody was waiting for us. Home, a place that no longer was, and never would be again.

Free?—Free? What were we freed for? Only to mourn and lament for the rest of our days the greatest tragedy that had ever befallen our people in our long and trying history.

THE MINUTES passed, and still we knelt. Then with common accord we rose from the ground. To me, it seemed that we had just arisen from *Shiva,* which is our traditional form of mourning. We ventured outside, where we found thousands of prisoners walking, dancing, marching in formation, singing, crying, and shouting in celebration.

By now the main body of tanks and armored vehicles had trundled well ahead, pushing and crushing the nation that had disgraced humanity to a just, final, and irrevocable defeat. Here and there, some prisoners, the old Buchenwaldians, were moving ahead and leaving by the main gate, armed with rifles and revolvers. Their faces were white masks, but their eyes burned with a fierce light. They were not trying to escape, nor were they intent on assisting the victorious Americans. Their one objective was to track down the murderous S.S. guards, those killers who in the hour of retribution had made a cowardly escape into the thick forest which lay close to the nearby city of Weimar. The pendulum had swung round, and now the prisoners were after the blood of their captors. Revenge, just punishment for the uniformed beasts who had slaughtered millions of innocent victims, was not to be denied.

As the avenging Buchenwaldians hurried out of the main gate, the first U.S. armored car drove into the camp proper. We rushed towards it, kissing, patting, and stroking its bullet-proof body, and when the first man, an officer, thrust his steel-helmeted head out of the turret, he was pulled out by the mass of men and lifted shoulder-high. Accompanied by jubilant thousands, he was carried about the camp despite his incessant protests and demands to be returned to his troops. He was hailed by the Buchenwald prisoners as the symbol of their freedom and victory.

The great day was drawing to its close. Darkness fell. By now the camp was in possession of about one hundred S.S. guards who had been dragged in by the armed inmates. Some still wore their hated uniform; others had already donned civilian clothes which they had prepared months ahead. These erstwhile Nazi bullies were confined to a separate block near the main gates, surrounded by a posse of armed *Haeftlinge*.

They cried like lost children, shouting and protesting their innocence to the angry mass of prisoners milling around the block. Some pleaded passionately that they had never been near the camp; others insisted that they were "only guards." The more inventive types claimed that their grandparents were Jews. Never has there been such a swing round from captor to captive.

When morning dawned, camp loudspeakers passed on their messages in a dozen languages, warning the liberated prisoners that the retreating S.S. had blown up the water system. It was an act of God that they did not manage to carry out their other projects, such as exploding the mines which were found all over the camp.

A week elapsed before the U.S. Army managed to take

[195]

charge of the camp, which included thousands of *Muselmaenner*—living corpses who were no longer able to move or even talk, so injured and seriously ill were they. Arrangements for food and water supply were made, and steps taken to dispose of the barrack full of captured S.S. men.

Buchenwald was a tragic and pitiful sight in these postwar days. Day after day, new pits and huts were discovered into which thousands of dead bodies had been dumped waiting to be taken to the camp's huge crematoria. The yards inside the crematoria were packed with huge piles of dead bodies stacked twenty feet high, while scores of blocks were filled to overflowing with *Muselmaenner,* the ghastly cripples and starved-out men whose only possible salvation was a mercifully quick death and burial.

Hundreds of prisoners who in their wild hunger had rushed the kitchens and stormed the food stores, died the next day sitting on the toilets or lying on their beds. Long, long after the Nazi captors had deserted their prisoners, death raged throughout the camp and took its toll in thousands. There seemed no end to the misery and wretchedness of Buchenwald. Liberation Day had brought its own tragic end, and it broke one's heart to see that now, when aid and assistance were beginning to arrive from all parts of the globe, for many thousands of prisoners, beyond human help, they had come too late.

Meanwhile, German civilians by the hundreds were brought in daily from the nearby city of Weimar. Their task was to work in the huge kitchens, to clean and disinfect the barracks, and to dig mass graves on a steep mountain slope which stood about a mile away from the camp, and which overlooked Weimar.

I picked up a few English words and commercialized them by becoming a guide and showing visiting troops over the death camp.

"May I show you the concentration camp?" I would ask the soldiers as they streamed through the main gates. Then I would guide them around the camp, beginning with the crematoria whose stoves still held charred but recognizable bodies, on to the hospital, the *Muselmaenner's* block, the punishment barracks, the dog kennels, and so on.

My reward consisted of cigarettes, chocolates, soft sweet biscuits, tinned food, and other delicious delicacies which I shared with Benzi, Grunwald, and other friends.

After "working" in the mornings, I would spend the afternoons at the cemetery watching over the Germans as they dug the graves, and myself joining other inmates who volunteered to assist in the burials.

Thousands of victims were literally chucked like old rags into the gaping mass-graves. There was no time for identification attempts or even for religious rituals, in spite of the tragic scenes that frequently occurred when inmates recognized their relatives or close friends among the mass of corpses, and prayed over them.

The worthiest service I could think of performing in this huge holocaust was to say a few words of prayer. It was, indeed, all I could hope to do. Each of my visits was concluded with a quiet recital of the traditional mourners' *Kaddish.*

"May His great Name be exalted and sanctified throughout the world. . . ."

As I walked back to the camp across the broad concrete roads, built in the center of the thick forest by Jewish blood and lives, I pondered the words of the *Kaddish.*

What would happen to our Jewish nation, to our religion and heritage, after this great and tragic disaster? The face of every Jewish inmate in the camp mirrored a vivid picture of the Jewish people: a crippled and shrunken people, a race which had suffered the most tremendous spiritual, as well as physical, onslaught in the history of mankind; a race of orphans, widows, and widowers; a race of mourning fathers who had lost their sons; of saddened mothers who had their babies snatched away from their breasts; of sons who had seen their fathers, brothers, and sisters burnt to ashes while still half alive.

We had not the heroic glamor of soldiers who had died on the battlefield, or sailors drowned in the ocean; we were prisoners who had been humiliated and scorned, and now that we were free, what did the future hold?

We had lost our noblest and finest, our dearest and most precious, in the course of a callously prepared program of cold murder, destruction, and annihilation; we were a nation whose blood was shed in every country under Nazi occupation, far away from battlefields and air attacks.

Who, I wondered, would again care to hear of God, of religion, of rituals, and of observances?

I knew that the Germans would now have to supply us with food, that the British would bring drugs and medical aid, that the Americans would flood us with cigarettes, chocolates, and vitamins. But who would provide the religious serum which was so necessary to instil some spirit of Godliness into a hopelessly crushed people?

I felt the great need of my father's guidance and precept to put me on my feet again. I needed him so much, for he always knew the answers to my problems. I felt sure that he would be able to assure me that there was still a God over us, that everything that I had learned to hold and treasure was still true. But my father was dead, burned by the Nazis. Yet even now I could feel his influence.

Now that the dreadful nightmare that had started at Sered had come to an end, I had to start life afresh. How would I fare? Where should I go? Certainly I could not stay in the Devil's Chambers of Buchenwald, nor could I face the vast unknown of a foreign land.

So it came that when I was asked by the authorities after V.E. Day whether I would like to return to Czechoslovakia or emigrate to the West, I decided to return home. Maybe there was still a very faint ray of hope in me that some of my kinsmen had managed to survive. I had met people who had saved themselves at the very gates of gas chambers. Could there be? . . . Perhaps? . . . Who knew?

There were my sisters, Paula and Golda. I cherished the hope that by some miracle they might have survived the holocaust inside their bunkers in Nitra, and that I would find them safe with their families.

Bratislava was the town of my birth and my youth—the place which I loved and for which I longed whenever I left it, even for a short trip; the place where I learned to become a Jew and suffered inhuman hardships for being one. This, I felt, was the only place where I could start my life again and face the future with hope and confidence.

But strangely enough it was on the pyre of the camp, in that hellhole of Buchenwald, that I received my first injection of vitamin R—Religious Revival.

A few days before our scheduled departure for Czechoslovakia, the camp loudspeakers blazed out an announcement that the Jewish chaplain to the U.S. forces would be conducting religious services in the evening to mark the festival of *Shavuoth*—the anniversary of the receiving of the Law by the Jewish people on Mount Sinai.

Having lost my handwritten diary, as well as my *Haggadah*, during the march from Nieder-Orschel to Buchenwald, this announcement came as a pleasant yet disturbing surprise.

Since my childhood I had always looked forward eagerly to the arrival of our wonderful and inspiring festivals, and particularly so in the tragic war years. But I wondered whether we weren't being put to a test too soon. Who among those thousands of physical and mental cripples would want to attend services and prayers so soon after their tragic experiences? The Festival of the Receiving of the *Torah!* Within a few weeks after liberation, religion which had seemed to do so little for us, was now challenging us and our loyalties.

But just as you cannot measure the physical strength of an oppressed people, so you cannot gauge its spiritual wealth and power.

On that evening, Buchenwald staged a fantastic demonstration of faith and loyalty to God. Thousands upon thousands of liberated Jews crowded into the specially vacated block for the first postwar Jewish religious service to be held on the soil of defeated Germany. The *Muselmaenner,* the cripples, the injured, and the weak came to demonstrate to the world that the last ounce of their strength, the last drop of their blood, and the last breath of their lives belonged to God, to *Torah,* and to the Jewish religion.

As Chaplain Schechter intoned the Evening Prayers, all the inmates in and outside the block stood in silence re-accepting the *Torah* whose people, message, and purpose Hitler's Germany had attempted to destroy. Jewish history repeated itself. Just as our forefathers who were liberated from Egypt accepted the Law in the desert, so did we, the liberated Jews of Buchenwald, reaccept the same Law in the concentration camps of Germany.

❖   ❖   ❖   ❖   ❖   ❖   ❖

CONCLUSION

OF THE eight hundred Slovakian Jews who were with me on
that journey from Sered to Auschwitz just ten months ago,
only a few score were with me on the transport back to Czechoslovakia. Benzi, Grunwald, Fischhof, Hugo Gross, Federweiss,
Schiff, and the other few survivors managed to accommodate
themselves on one army lorry, leaving the rest of the thirty-
truck convoy to be occupied in the main by non-Jewish, Czech
political prisoners.

The moment I set foot on Bratislavian soil, after a long and
tiresome journey in overcrowded railway wagons, I realized
that it was no longer the place for me. It was no longer my
home. Oh yes, there were still the same streets, the familiar
tramcars, the well-known buildings, and the beloved houses.
But that was all. Bratislava, as I knew it and remembered it
in my heart, was gone forever. I felt like a man poking in the
ruins of his home which had been destroyed by an earthquake.
He would find in it oddments and remnants which would only
serve to bring tears to his eyes and painful memories to his

heart. He might find his wife's wedding photograph—but not his wife. He would pull out of the ruins his baby's favorite doll—but not the child.

A few of the familiar objects in my former home were still there. But those who brought life and love into them were missing. Yet I found great joy in discovering that my sisters in Nitra had indeed managed to save their families, and in the knowledge that my brothers, too, were safe in England.

With the handful of my friends who had trickled back from the concentration camps, we established a home for ourselves in the once popular Judengasse.

We labored long and earnestly to restore Bratislava to at least some of its former beauty and glory as a center of Jewry and Jewish life. But even the most hopeful and optimistic of us soon realized that all our efforts would be in vain. We had survived the blood orgy of the creed of Nazism, we had done our duty to help in the rebuilding of our people, but a new world had been born while we languished in the devil's chambers, and we could not hope to resurrect the old one. That had died with Nazism.

The world of Hitler was assuredly dead, but the powers of terror, hatred, and oppression which he had invented still existed as small but very dangerous volcanoes which might erupt at any place, and at any time.

I, and indeed most of the other repatriates sadly left Bratislava again—this time for good. We had paid too high a price for our lives and for our religion to risk losing them again.

The world war of the nations was over, but that of the individual was just beginning. I had to be sure to fight mine on safe ground, for victory was still in the balance. Sick with remembered pain that would increase with the years, I turned my face to the West. Would it offer me what I so sorely needed?

GLOSSARY

ALEPH-BES or BET	The Hebrew alphabet.
ARBAH MINIM	Four species used in the ritual during the Feast or Festival of Tabernacles.
AVINU MALKENU	Part of the Holy Days' Prayers—prayer of supplication.
EKHAH	Book of Lamentations.
ETROG	See Arbah Minim.
HAGGADAH	Book read on the first two nights of Passover, containing the story of the Exodus from Egypt.
HALLEL	Psalms of praise recited on Festivals and on the first day of the month.
HALLAH	Plaited loaves of bread eaten on the Sabbath and Festivals or Holy Days.
HANUKKAH	Eight-day celebration or Festival of Lights commemorating the miraculous victory of the Jews over their Greek oppressors.
HESHVAN	Second month of the Jewish religious calendar year, and eighth month of the Jewish civil calendar year.
KADDISH	Mourners' prayer.

KIDDUSH	Benediction of sanctification recited on Sabbath and Festivals or Holy Days.
LULAV	Palm-branch taken on the Feast of Tabernacles.
MAZKIR	Memorial prayer for the dead.
MAOZ TZUR	Traditional Hanukkah hymn.
MATZAH	Unleavened bread eaten on Passover.
MENORAH	Eight-branched lamp used on Hanukkah.
OLAM HABA	"The World to Come."
ONO HASHEM HOSHIO NO	"Please, oh Lord, help!"
PASSOVER	First of three festivals of pilgrimage to Jerusalem.
PESACH	The Passover.
ROSH HODESH	First day of the month.
ROSH HASHANAH	Jewish New Year. First day of the seventh month.
SEDER	Home celebration, first night of Passover.
SABBATH BERESHIT	First Sabbath after Festivals when the first chapters of Genesis are read in the synagogue.
SHAVUOTH	Feast of Weeks, or Pentecost.
SHAHARIT	Morning prayer.
SHALOM ALEIKHEM	The usual Jewish greeting.
SHEMA YISRAEL	Judaism's confession of faith. First words of prayer proclaiming the unity of God.
SHEVAT, 15th of	"New Year of Trees" celebration.
SHIVA	The seven days of mourning, following burial of a relative.
SIMHAT TORAH	The last day of Sukkot on which the reading of the five books of Moses is completed.
SUKKOT	Feast of Tabernacles, one of three pilgrim Festivals.

SUKKAH	Booth erected for the Feast of Tabernacles.
TALLIT	Prayer shawl.
TEFILLIN	Phylacteries worn during the morning weekday services.
TISHA B'AV	Day commemorating the destruction of the First and Second Temples.
TORAH	The Pentateuch, or "Law of Moses," or "the Written Law."
YOM KIPPUR	Day of Atonement.